A History of the Armenian People

A History of the Armenian People

Volume I:
Pre-History to 1500 A.D.

George A. Bournoutian

MAZDA PUBLISHERS

Costa Mesa, California

The publication of this volume was made possible by a grant from the
AGBU Alex Manoogian Cultural Fund

Library of Congress Cataloging-in-Publication Data

Bournoutian, George A.
  A history of the Armenian people / George A. Bournoutian.
    p.   cm.
  Includes bibliographical references and index.
  Contents: v. 1. Pre-history to 1500 A.D.
    1. Armenia — History.
  DS175.B65   1993
  966.6'2 — dc20   92-39705
                                                                                    CIP

ISBN: 0-939214-96-2
10 9 8 7 6 5 4 3 2

MAZDA PUBLISHERS 1995

To Sahak of Van and Haikanoush of Gandzak

Contents

MAPS

TIME-LINES

PLATES

Preface

For the past seventeen years I have taught surveys of Armenian history at various colleges, universities, and community centers throughout the United States and Canada. Many attending these lectures have repeatedly remarked upon the lack of a suitable volume covering the history of the Armenians in English. Some suggested that I collect my notes into such a book. I hesitated primarily because I was aware of the preparation of two forthcoming scholarly and detailed collections on the history of the Armenian people, to which I have contributed chapters. Some years ago, however, I began teaching a number of courses on world civilization and discovered that most high school and college world history texts do not mention the Armenians at all. The few that do, include but a brief a mention of the Armenians. Only a limited number of students have a chance to take Armenian history courses either in high school or in college. Only a handful of universities offer Armenian history courses, and, unless students attend American-Armenian schools, most will not learn much about Armenian history. Moreover, American-Armenian schools continue to teach Armenian history either as a collection of stories and legends or as a distinct phenomenon unrelated to the rest of the world events.

It was Louise Manoogian Simone, the President of the Armenian General Benevolent Union, who suggested that I write a brief but concise volume which would enable Armenian and non-Armenian students to place the history of Armenia and its people in relation to that of the rest

xi

of the world. To accomplish this I have decided to approach this book as a supplement which follows the historical chronology of a number of major texts on world civilizations used around the country. Following their example, I have divided the work into two volumes, pre-1500 and post-1500. I have also included time-lines, photos, and maps to help students correlate Armenian history with the history text used in their particular institution.

The present work does not pretend to be original scholarly research based on archival sources. It contains, however, some fresh interpretations of Armenian historical traditions and has utilized numerous primary and secondary sources. It is intended mainly for college undergraduates, although high school seniors and their instructors, as well as the general public will benefit from it as well. Its primary purpose is to familiarize Armenian and non-Armenian students with a people and culture which is very much absent from most history courses and texts. The work does not address every issue of the extremely complicated history of Armenia, but rather concentrates on its political history. Some material has been simplified and condensed, and a number of dates used are still disputed by scholars.

A work of this nature owes much to many. Dr. Rouben Adalian of the Armenian Assembly lent invaluable insight through his objective criticism. Dr. Robert Hewsen of Glassboro State College kindly provided a number of maps and other geographical data. Dr. Krikor Maksoudian of the Zohrab Center of the Armenian Diocese clarified several theological questions. Dr. Ehsan Yarshater of the Iran Center of Columbia University provided details on the various scripts used in ancient Armenia. Aram Arkun of the Zohrab Center, Rosalyn Ashby of Yavapai College, Dr. Richard Guidorizzi and Dr. Dennis Schmidt, both of Iona College read the manuscript and made useful suggestions. I would like to thank Roxanna Glass for her editorial efforts, Ann Cammett for the preparation of the maps and time-lines, the secretarial services of Iona College for their assistance, and Ara Kalaydjian of the *Armenian Mirror Spectator* for providing the plates. I would also like to express my gratitude to my teacher, Professor Richard Hovannisian of UCLA, whose fascinating lectures have inspired so many students to search for the answers we are still seeking in Armenian history. I also wish to thank

Louise Simone for her moral support and Edmond Azadian and the AGBU Alex Manoogian Cultural Fund for their financial assistance. There is one person, however, without whose help the present volume would have not materialized and to whom I am especially indebted: my wife, Ani, a historian in her own right, who took care of two children and still managed to infuse her energy and objectivity into the final draft.

George A. Bournoutian
Associate Professor of History, Iona College
1993

Explanatory Notes

DATING SYSTEM

In an effort to provide a true world perspective and eliminate a seeming Christian or Western bias, a few college texts have decided to substitute B.C.E. (Before the Common Era) for B.C. (Before Christ) and C.E. (Common Era) for A.D. (Anno Domini). Since this concept has not yet been universally adopted, I have decided to retain the B.C. and A.D. designations in the text and add B.C.E. and C.E. in the time-lines. It is important to note, however, that various cultures have different calendars. The Armenian Church calendar, for example, differs by some 550 years from the calendar used in the Western world today. Chinese, Hebrew, Arab, Iranian, and pre-revolutionary Russian calendars, among others, also differ from our calendar. To simplify matters, all dates have been converted to the dating system used in the West.

In addition, it should be noted that there are no exact dates for some historical occurrences or reigns of various rulers in ancient times. In such cases an approximate date or *circa*, abbreviated as *c.*, is used. All dates following the names of rulers or popes refer to their reigns; in all other cases they refer to life span.

GEOGRAPHICAL TERMS

Another attempt to correct any Eurocentric bias has been to alter some, but not all, commonly-used geographical terms. Thus instead of *Middle East, Near East,* or the *Levant,* some historians now use the more accurate term, *Western Asia; Far East* or the *Orient* has sometimes been replaced by *East Asia;* the Indian subcontinent is referred to as *South Asia; Transcaucasia* is occasionally called *eastern Caucasus.* Here too, the concept has not been universally accepted and I shall, therefore, retain geographical terms of the past or, in some instances, as they are currently used in the news media. The term *Islamic Middle East,* therefore, includes the present-day territories of Persia or Iran, Egypt, Syria, Turkey, Lebanon, Iraq, Jordan, Palestine, Kuwait, Saudi Arabia, Yemen, and the various Persian Gulf states. *Asia Minor* or *Anatolia* refers to the territory of present-day Turkey. *Transcaucasia* refers to the present-day republics of Armenia, Georgia, and Azerbaijan. *Mesopotamia* refers to the territory of present-day Iraq. The *Balkans* refers to the present-day states of Greece, Albania, Bulgaria, Romania and Yugoslavia. The *Levant* encompasses mainly Lebanon and parts of the coastal lands of Syria and Israel. *Azerbaijan* refers to Persian Azerbaijan, or the territory in northwestern Iran below the Arax river.

TRANSLITERATION

To conform with the spoken language in the Republic of Armenia, Armenian words, with minor exceptions, have been transliterated according to sounds of Eastern Armenian. The Persian words are transliterated according to the sounds of modern Persian. A simplified transliteration system with no diacritical marks or ligatures has been utilized in both instances. Some of the foreign names and terms, particularly those included in the *Webster's Unabridged Dictionary,* have been Anglicized, while others have retained their original form. Finally, the Latinized version, if any, of Armenian names or variations of common names will appear in parentheses.

SOURCES

In addition to the sources listed in the bibliographical guide, I have relied on my lecture notes and have benefitted from class notes on Armenian history courses taught by Richard G. Hovannisian at UCLA and Nina G. Garsoian at Columbia University. Moreover, I have consulted the following world history texts, encyclopedias, and atlases for the chronology and the preparation of the time-lines and maps.

World History Texts

A. Esler, *The Human Venture: A World History from Prehistory to the Present*. 2nd Edition (Prentice Hall, New Jersey, 1992).

A. M. Craig, W. A. Graham, D. Kagan et. al. eds., *The Heritage of World Civilizations*. 2nd Edition (Macmillan, New York, 1990). R. L. Greaves, R. Zaller et. al. eds., *Civilizations of the World*. (Harper and Row, New York, 1990).

J. P. McKay, B. D. Hill, J. Buckler et. al. eds., *A History of World Societies*. 3rd Edition (Houghton Mifflin, Boston, 1992).

W. H. McNeill, *A History of the Human Community*. 3rd Edition (Prentice Hall, New Jersey, 1990).

P. L. Ralph, R. E. Lerner, E. M. Burns, et al. eds., *World Civilizations*. 8th Edition (W. W. Norton Co., New York), 1991.

L. S. Stavrianos, *A Global History*. 5th Edition (Prentice Hall, New Jersey, 1991).

J. Upshur, J. Terry, J. Holoka et. al. eds., *World History*. (West Publishing Company, Los Angeles, 1991).

T. W. Wallbank, A. M. Taylor, et. al. eds., *Civilizations Past and Present*. 7th Edition (Harper Collins, New York, 1992).

R. W. Winks, C. Brinton, et al. eds., *A History of Civilization* (Prentice Hall, New Jersey, 1992).

Encyclopedias

Encyclopaedia Iranica. Ehsan Yarshater editor. Center for Iranian Studies, Columbia University, New York (Routledge and Kegan Paul, London).

J. A. Garraty and P. Gay eds., *The Columbia History of the World* (Harper & Row, New York, 1981).

W. L. Langer, *An Encyclopedia of World History*. 5th Edition (Houghton Mifflin, Boston, 1972).

Soviet Armenian Encyclopedia. Academy of Sciences of Armenia, Yerevan (in Armenian).

Atlases

G. Armen, V. Artinian, H. Abdalian, *Historical Atlas of Armenia* (New York, 1987).
Hammond Historical Atlas of the World (Maplewood, N. J., 1989).
C. McEvedy, *The Penguin Atlas of Ancient History* (Baltimore, 1968).
C. McEvedy, *The Penguin Atlas of Medieval History* (New York, 1987).
'A. Mostoufi, et al. eds. *Historical Atlas of Iran* (Tehran, 1971).

Photos

S. Der Nersessian, *Armenian Art.*
D.M. Lang, *Armenia, Cradle of Civilization.*

Introduction

In their nearly 3000-year history, the Armenians have rarely played the role of aggressor; rather, they have excelled in agriculture, arts and crafts, and trade. Armenians have produced unique architectural monuments, sculpture, illuminated manuscripts, literature, and philosophical and legal tracts. Moreover, a number of important philosophical and scientific works have survived only in their Armenian translations. In addition, the Armenians, because of their location and participation in international trade, have contributed to the cultural and scientific development of both the East and the West. College graduates and even teachers, however, know very little about the Armenians or their history. Historians have concentrated their research on the record of conquerors, who through military, economic or cultural invasions have dominated or destroyed smaller nations. Thus, despite their accomplishments, the Armenians have been given less space in general history texts than Attila the Hun.

To be sure, the history of Armenia is a difficult one to reconstruct, for several reasons. Sources written before the invention of the Armenian alphabet in the fifth century A.D., require a familiarity with Aramaic, Greek, Middle Persian and Syriac. Later sources require a knowledge of Arabic, Latin, Georgian, Turkish, Modern Persian, Mongolian, Russian, French, and Italian, as well as classical and modern Armenian. Valuable historical evidence has no doubt been destroyed by the numerous invasions of and earthquakes in the Armenian homeland. Furthermore, the modern political divisions of historical Armenia among neighboring states have made archival and archeological research a sensitive, and often difficult, task. Moreover, the systematic application of modern historical research techniques to the study of Armenian history is but a recent phenomenon.

Armenia is one of the few small nations which managed to survive repeated invasions, destruction, and persecution. The Armenians have been described through the centuries as adaptable, resilient, enterprising, and steadfast. How they managed to survive while larger and more powerful states disappeared, and how, at the same time, they were able to make significant contributions to world civilization, is the history of the Armenian people.

I

Highlands and Crossroads:
The Land of Armenia

Armenia is a landlocked mountainous plateau with an average height of 5000 feet above sea level. The Armenian highlands stretch roughly between 38° and 48° longitude East and 37.5° and 41.5° latitude North and cover an area of some 125,000 square miles. In present-day terms, historic Armenia comprises most of eastern Turkey, the northeastern corner of Iran, parts of the Azerbaijan and Georgian Republics, as well as the entire territory of the Armenian Republic, and is defined by a number of natural boundaries. The Kur River separates the Armenian highlands in the east from the lowlands which adjoin the Caspian Sea. The Pontic range, which joins the Lesser Caucasus mountain chain, separates Armenia from the Black Sea and Georgia, forming the northern boundary. The Taurus Mountains, which join the upper Zagros chain and the Iranian plateau, form the southern boundary of Armenia and separate it from Syria, Kurdistan and Iran. The western boundary of Armenia has generally been the Euphrates River and the northern stretch of the Anti-Taurus Mountains. Armenians have also established communities east of the Kur, as far as the Caspian Sea, and states west of the Euphrates, as far as Cilicia, on the Mediterranean Sea.

Some fifty million years ago, the geological structure of Armenia went through many phases, creating great mountains and high, now-inactive volcanic peaks throughout the plateau. The larger peak of Mount Ararat (16,946 feet), Mount Sipan (14,540 feet), Mount Aragads (13,410 feet), the smaller peak of Mount Ararat (12,839 feet), and Mount Bingol

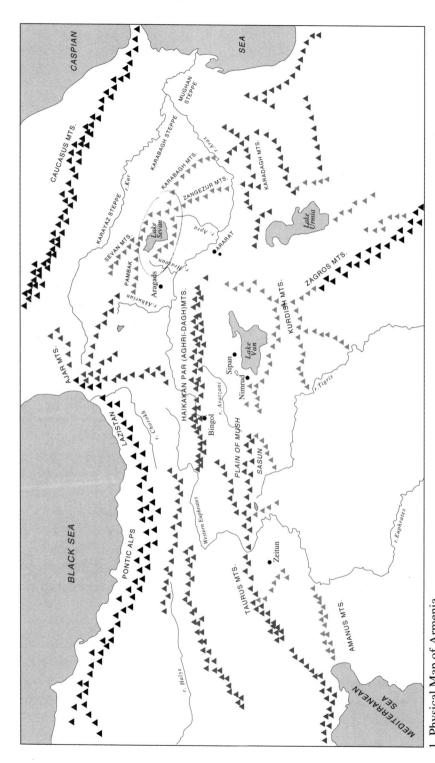

1. Physical Map of Armenia

(10,770 feet), from which the Arax and the Euphrates rivers originate, are examples. A number of mountain chains within Armenia divide the plateau into distinct regions, a phenomenon which has had significant political and historical ramifications. The many mountains are the source of numerous rivers, all unnavigable, which have created deep gorges, ravines and waterfalls. Of these rivers, the longest is the Arax, which starts in the mountains of eastern Anatolia and, after joining the Kur river, empties into the Caspian Sea. The Arax flows through and fertilizes the plain of Ararat and the Arax valley. The Euphrates, another important river, was the ancient boundary dividing what became Lesser and Greater Armenia. A number of other rivers, among them the Kur and the Tigris, flow briefly through Armenia. A number of lakes are situated in the Armenian highlands, the most important of which is Lake Van in present-day Turkey. The deepest lake, it also has a high borax content. Lake Sevan, which is the highest in elevation (over 6300 feet above sea level), is in the present-day Armenian Republic. Lake Urmia (Urmiye), in present-day Iran, is the shallowest and extremely salty (see map 1).

Armenia lies in the temperate zone and has a variety of climates. In general, winters are long and can be severe, while summers are usually short and very hot. Some plains, because of their lower altitudes, are better suited for agriculture, and have fostered population centers throughout the centuries. The variety of temperatures has enabled the land to support a great diversity of *flora* and *fauna* common to Western Asia and Transcaucasia. The mountains also supply abundant deposits of mineral ores, including copper, iron, zinc, lead, silver, and gold. There are also large salt mines as well as borax, obsidian and volcanic tufa stone. The generally dry Armenian climate has necessitated artificial irrigation throughout history. In fact, the soil, which is volcanic, is quite fertile and, with sufficient water, capable of intensive farming. Farming is prevalent in the lower altitudes, while nomadism is practiced in the highlands. Although Armenians have been known as artisans and merchants, the majority of Armenians, until recently, were primarily engaged in agriculture. In addition to cereal crops, Armenia grew vegetables, various oil seeds, and, especially, fruit. Armenian fruit has been famous from ancient times, with the pomegranate and apricot, referred to by the Romans as the *Armenian plum*, being the most renowned. Lying on the Anatolian fault, the Armenian plateau is subject to seismic tremors. Major earthquakes have been recorded there since the ninth century, some of which have destroyed entire cities. The most recent earthquake in the region, that of 7 December 1988, killed some thirty thousand people and leveled numerous communities.

Geography has determined the history of many nations and no where is this more true than in Armenia. Unlike Japan and England, which were geographically isolated and rarely faced invasions, Armenia's location made it a link between neighboring empires. As a bridge between Asia and Europe for trade as well as culture, Armenia's position allowed its people to enrich themselves materially and culturally by absorbing and adapting the knowledge of much of the civilized world. In return, Armenians became the catalyst which enabled Europe to learn from Asia during the ancient and medieval periods, and Asia from Europe, in modern times. While Armenia's mountain boundaries generally protected it in the north and south, the river valleys and other passageways left its eastern and western borders less secure. Holding a unique position between Asia and Europe, Armenia was a corridor which frequently attracted invaders and resulted in long periods of foreign domination. Many of its small and large neighbors disappeared from history, but Armenia and its people managed to survive. Ironically, the same landscape which invited destruction was also partially responsible for preserving its inhabitants. The numerous mountain chains, which divided Armenia into valleys, prevented it from achieving a united state under a strong centralized ruler during much of its history. This very fact, however, was a blessing in disguise, for, unlike a highly centralized state, such as Assyria, whose entire culture vanished with the collapse of its capital city, Armenia's lack of political unity meant the survival of its culture even while its kings were deposed and its capital cities destroyed.

B.C.E.	ARMENIA	FERTILE CRESCENT & EGYPT	CRETE / GREECE	INDIA & CHINA	THE AMERICAS
c.400,000 to 7000	The Old Stone Age (Paleolithic). Crude tools made from flint and black volcanic rock (obsidian). Evidence of modern man (40,000 B.C.), discovery of fire, hunting and food gathering. Early communal organizations, some along matriarchal lines, develop by 12,000 B.C. Agricultural experiments with wild grains during the Middle Stone Age (Mesolithic.)				
c.7000 to 3200	The New Stone Age (Neolithic). The end of the last ice-age. Sedentary life begins, tilling the soil, cultivation of plants, domestication of animals, more sophisticated stone tools. After 5,000 B.C., some use of copper during the Copper-Stone Age (Chalcolithic). Nomadic life continues in many regions, agricultural settlements rise in other regions. Some walled villages/towns appear. Beginning of divisions of labor, appearence of textiles, woven baskets and jewelry.				
3200	The Bronze Age. Invention of the wheel, plows with wooden shares, bronze weapons, utensils and tools. Use of animals in agriculture, large-scale irrigation projects and major agricultural developments, rise of cities, writing systems, and recorded history.				
3000	Metal-working in Caucasus (c. 3000)	Sumerian civilization Lunar calendar, early religions, ziggurats, cuneiform script (c. 3200-3000) Egypt unified, first pyramid, hieroglyphics (c. 3100-2770)		Indus Valley civilization (c. 3000-1600) Early urban civilization in China (c. 3000-1800)	Early pottery in Ecuador (c. 3000)
		Old Kingdom, Egypt (c. 2770-2200)			
2500		Akkadian Empire (c. 2370-2200)		Domestication of horses Silkworm cultivation in China (c. 2500) Mohenjo-Daro and Harappa settlements in India (c. 2500-1500)	
	Hurrians (c. 2300)	Sumerian revival (c. 2200-2000)			
2000		Middle Kingdom, Egypt (c. 2050-1786) Solar calendar Belief of personal immortality in religion			

Table 1: Pre-History to 1000 B.C.

B.C.E.	ARMENIA	FERTILE CRESCENT & EGYPT	CRETE / GREECE	INDIA & CHINA	THE AMERICAS
2000	Guti (c. 2000)	Old Babylonian Empire (c. 2000-1600)	Minoan civilization in Knossos, Crete (c. 2000-1500)		Metal-working in Peru (c. 2000)
	Kassites (c. 1900)	Gilgamesh Epic	Greek Bronze Age (c. 2000-1500)	Shang Dynasty in China (c. 1766-1123)	
		Horses domesticated		Ideograghic script developed in China	
		Code of Hammurabi (c. 1770)			
	Indo-European invasions (c. 1700-1500)	Hyskos invasion/rule of Egypt (c. 1750-1560)			
		New Kingdom, Egypt (c. 1550-1087)	Mycenean civilization in Greece (c. 1600-1200)		
		Hittite Empire (c. 1500-1200)			
		Phoenicians develop first alphabet	Mycene dominates Crete (c. 1500-1400)	Aryan invasions of India (c. 1500)	
	Mitanni (c. 1600-1400)	Akhenaton's new religion, Egypt (c. 1375)	Minoan civilization ends (c. 1400)	Oldest Sanskrit literature in India	
		Assyrian Kingdom formed (c. 1300)		Early Vedas (Rig Veda) (c. 1500-1000)	
		Moses unites Jews in the worship of Yahweh (c. 1250)			
		Rise of Assyria			
		Shalmaneser I (c. 1274-1245)			
	Federations of Hayasa, Azzi, Arme-Shupria, and Uruatri formed in the region (c. 1300-900)	Collapse of Hittite Empire (c. 1200)	Trojan War and the collapse of Mycene (c. 1180-1100)		Olmec civilization in San Lorenzo, Mexico (c. 1200-900)
		Hebrews occupy Canaan			
		Period of Judges (c. 1200-1025)			
		Trojan War (c. 1180)			
		Tiglath-pileser I (c. 1115-1077)			
1100 Iron Age		Shalmaneser II (c. 1031-1020)	Greek Dark Ages (c. 1100-800)	Chou Dynasty (c. 1100-256)	
		Decline of Assyria (c. 1020-900)			
		United Jewish State (1025-933)			

Table 1: Pre-History to 1000 B.C.

B.C.E.	ARMENIA	MIDDLE EAST, PERSIA & EGYPT	GREECE & ROME	INDIA, CHINA & JAPAN	SUB-SAHARAN AFRICA & THE AMERICAS
1000	Iron-working in Transcaucasia	Libyan and Nubian rulers in Egypt (c. 1000-700) Kingdom of Israel (933-722) Kingdom of Judah (933-586)	Greek Dark Ages (c. 1100-800)	Chou Dynasty continues (c. 1100-256) Late Vedas (c. 1100-500) Emergence of caste system (c. 1000)	
900	Urartu emerges as a rival of Assyria Arame (c. 870-845) Sarduri I (c. 845-825) Tushpa built (c. 840) Shalmaneser invades Urartu (841) Ispuini (c. 825-810)	Revival of Assyria (c. 900-745) Ashur-nasirpal (c. 884-859) Shalmaneser III (c. 860-824)			Iron working fosters population centers in Africa Olmec center moved to La Vente in Tabasco, Mexico
800	Menua (c. 810-785) Argishti I (c. 785-760) Erebuni built (c. 782) Argistihinili built (c. 775) Apex of Urartu Sarduri II (c. 760-735) Tiglath-pileser invades Urartu (744) Loss of Syria (c. 735) Rusa I (735-714) Cimmerian invasions Sargon's invasion 714 Argishti II (c. 714-685)	Rise of Media Assyria rules parts of Egypt (c. 740-705) Tiglath-pileser III (c. 745-727) Assyrian Empire (c. 750-700) Sargon II (c. 722-705) Cimmerian invasions	Rise of Athens and Sparta (c. 800) Iliad & Odyssey (c. 750) Rome founded (c. 750) Expansion of Greek colonies (c. 750-600) Rise of Greek land-owning class (c. 750 - 600)	Upanishads (c. 800-600) Foundation of Hinduism Feudalism in China (c. 800-250)	Kush Kingdom founded in Africa (c. 800)
700	Scythian invasions Rusa II (c. 685-645) Teishebaini built (c. 650) Erimena (c. 625-615) Decline of Urartu (615-610)	Kushites conquer and unite Egypt (c. 700-525) Ashur-banipal II (c. 688-624) Fall of Elam Zoroaster (c. 650) Rise of Persia (c. 650-550) Fall of Assyria (612-610) New Babylonian Empire (612-539) Medes form empire (612-550)	Age of tyrants in Greece (c. 650-500) Doric architectural style in Greece (c. 650-500) Thales of Miletus (c. 640-546)	Legendary beginning of current line of Japanese emperors (c. 650)	Height of ancient Ethiopian culture Olmec pyramids in Mexico

Table 2: 1000 B.C. to 600 B.C.

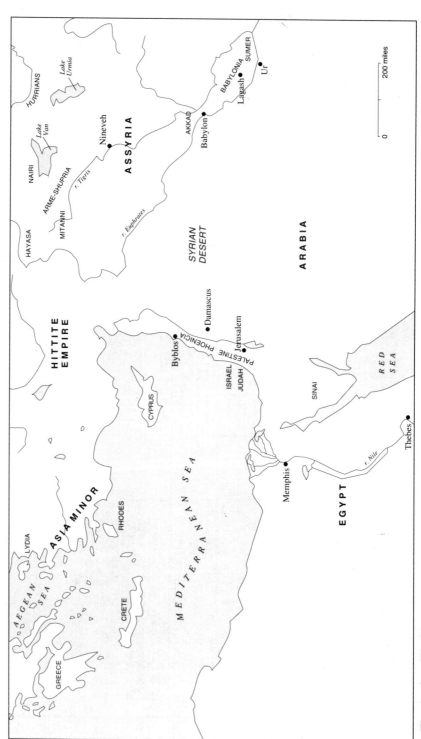

2. The Ancient World

II

Ara and Semiramis:

Urartu, the First Kingdom in Armenia (c. 870-590 B.C.)

The territory of historic Armenia, together with Mesopotamia, was one of the earliest regions to possess incipient agriculture — a stage in history when man began to replace the hunting and food-gathering of the Old and Middle Stone Ages with the food producing of the New Stone-Age period. Soon after, the use of copper began in the region and for the next two millennia remained confined to eastern Anatolia, Transcaucasia, Mesopotamia and Egypt. By 3000 B.C. the Mesopotamians had developed bronze, an alloy of copper and tin, which was soon adopted by the inhabitants of the Caucasus as well. Settlements, agriculture, and the use of metal utensils made Transcaucasia and Asia Minor not only one of the cradles of civilization, but gave it wealth and made it attractive to invaders. Between 3000 and 1500 B.C. Indo-European tribes, who had concentrated around the Aral, Caspian, Aegean, and Black Sea regions learned the art of making iron and began to move into the older and richer regions of the ancient world. The Indo-European Iranians from Asia and the Indo-European Hittites from Europe entered Transcaucasia and Asia Minor, respectively (There are recent studies which argue that the Indo-Europeans originated in Transcaucasia, from where they gradually spread to Asia and Europe; see chapter III). The Iranians confronted the indigenous Caucasian groups such as the Hurrians, Guti, and Kassites, and by 1500 B.C. the Indo-European Mitanni had created a kingdom in the region, introducing their language and deities. Simultaneously, the Hittites created a kingdom in Asia Minor which, by 1300 B.C., had developed into an empire stretching to the Euphrates River. At the same time, the Semitic Assyrians established a small kingdom in the south and slowly began to intermingle with or replace the older Semitic cultures of Mesopotamia. The Caucasian and Indo-European groups in eastern Anatolia and Transcaucasia eventually mixed, forming federations which traded with or fought the Hittites and Assyrians. Records from the Hittite king Suppiluliumas (c. 1388-1347 B.C.) and the Assyrian ruler Tiglath-pileser I (c. 1115-1077 B.C.) were among those who referred to these federations as the people of Hayasa-Azzi, Nairi, Arme-Shupria, and Uruatri, among others (see map 2). By 1200 B.C. the Hittite empire had collapsed and was replaced by the Phrygians and other Indo-Europeans from Thrace, while the Assyrian kingdom had gone into a period of hibernation.

The Origins of Urartu

The absence of a dominant state in the region allowed the amalgamated Caucasian and Indo-European groups to absorb or unite the smaller tribes and to create a large and powerful confederation. The dawn of the Iron Age around 1100 B.C., in the same region which had produced the Bronze Age, permitted the forging of new weapons and tools and facilitated the emergence of such a confederation. Soon after, the Urartians, who called themselves Biainili and who were probably of Hurrian stock, began to dominate, and by the ninth century B.C. they had formed the first kingdom in the region that later became known as Armenia.

The period of the kingdom of Urartu, also referred to by some historians as the kingdom of Van, witnessed a number of new developments around the world. Greece emerged from its dark ages and gave birth to Athens and Sparta. The *Iliad* and the *Odyssey* were composed and the Doric architectural style was developed. Zoroaster began to preach his message in Persia (Iran). Egypt lost its ancient glory and was dominated by Libyan, Nubian, Assyrian, and finally Kushite kings. In India, the *Upanishads* were written, Hinduism emerged, and the caste system was formulated. Feudalism developed in China, while the Olmec civilization flourished in Mexico.

Urartu as the Rival of Assyria

The formation of Urartu also corresponded with the resurgence of the Assyrian kingdom in the ninth century B.C. In fact, much of the data on Urartu comes from this neighbor and adversary. The first mention of the Urartian kingdom is by the Assyrian king Ashur-nasirpal (c. 884-859 B.C.), who campaigned there. For the next three centuries, Assyria and Urartu fought each other, with Assyria having limited success but never managing totally to subjugate its neighbor. Urartu was ultimately responsible for halting the Assyrian expansion into Anatolia, northern Persia, and Transcaucasia. One may view the history of the kingdom of Urartu as part of the struggle between Indo-European and Semitic groups of the area. In some regions, the two united to form new states; in others, cultural, linguistic, and religious differences resulted in long conflicts. With the exception of China, the entire Eurasian world was in a period of transition. In the end, the Indo-Europeans became dominant and created the classical civilizations of Greece, Persia, and India.

The first Urartian king, mentioned by the Assyrian king Shalmaneser III (c. 860-825 B.C.), was Arame or Aramu who ruled in the first half of the ninth century B.C.. If it was Arame who managed to organize a united kingdom, it was Sarduri or Sardure I (c. 845-825 B.C.) who should be credited for establishing a dynasty which would last until the end the early sixth century B.C. His first action was to build the capital city of Tushpa (present-day Van), on the eastern shore of Lake Van. The height of Urartian power was formed during the reigns of Ispuini (c. 825-810 B.C.), Menua (c. 810-785 B.C.), Argishti I (c. 785-753 B.C.) and his son Sarduri II (c. 753-735 B.C.). The brief decline of Assyria at the end of the ninth century assured Urartu's dominance of the region. By the eighth century B.C. the kingdom of Urartu stretched from the Euphrates in the west, the Caspian lowlands in the east, the shores of Lake Urmia in the south, and the Caucasus in the north — or basically the territory of what would later be Greater Armenia. Small cities, forts and many Urartian settlements were recorded by the Assyrians in their numerous campaigns. Large irrigation canals, some of which are still in use today, were constructed by Menua. Vineyards, orchards and various grains were also planted, and Urartu became a food-producing region. The availability of copper and iron and the early knowledge of iron-working enabled artisans to produce various bronze and iron weapons and other objects for war and trade.

The result of all this activity was an increase in population. It was at this time that the city of Musasir, west of Lake Urmia, was conquered by the Urartians and was made the religious center of the kingdom. The Urartians managed to defeat Assyria in a number of wars, take booty and prisoners, and to extend their domination over northern Syria. The Urartians built a number of forts to defend their kingdom from nomadic and Assyrian invasions. Argishti I founded the two most important bastions. In 782 B.C., on the plain of Ararat, he built the Erebuni (in Armenian, Arin-berd) fortress. This was the predecessor of the present-day city of Yerevan, making it one of the oldest continuously-inhabited urban centers in the world. In 775 B.C., west of Yerevan, on the bank of the Arax river, he constructed Argishtihinili (the modern Armavir). (See map 3.)

The reigns of Tiglath-pileser III (c. 745-727 B.C.) and Sargon II (c. 722-705 B.C.) not only halted Assyria's decline but transformed it into an empire which managed to penetrate much of Urartu, destroy and loot its cities, and take prisoners. Sargon employed a network of spies who reported on his northern neighbor. Some of these reports have survived, enabling historians to piece together some of the events which occurred at that time. They state that the Urartian rulers had to fight both the Assyrians and the Cimmerians, who were invading from the north. By 714 B.C., both of the invaders had destroyed parts of Urartu, forcing King Rusa I (c. 735-714 B.C.) to commit suicide. Urartu had acted as a buffer zone for the Cimmerian invaders, however, and once Urartu was weakened, the Cimmerians poured into Anatolia and Syria, and attacked Assyria.

Decline of Urartu

The seventh century B.C. witnessed the gradual rise of a new Babylonian state, and a minor revival in Egypt, as well as the emergence of Indo-European power centers in Persia. Urartu and Assyria, both in decline, made peace with each other and tried to cope with the

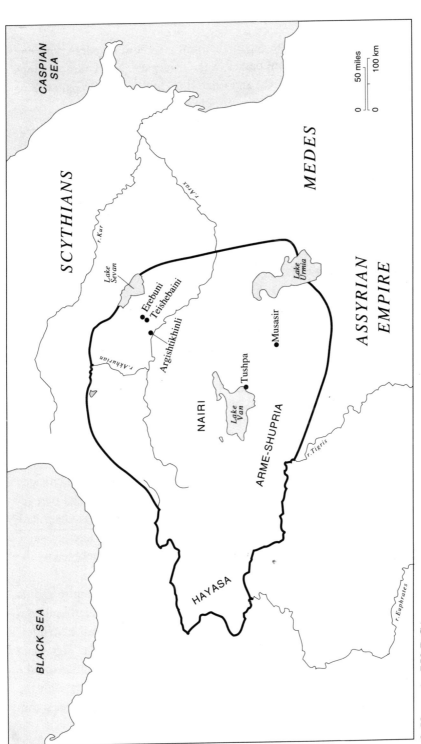

3. Urartu (c. 750 B.C.)

Map labels:

CASPIAN SEA

SCYTHIANS

MEDES

ASSYRIAN EMPIRE

BLACK SEA

r. Kur

r. Araxi

Lake Sevan

Lake Urmia

Erebuni
Teishebaini

Argishtikhinili

r. Akhurian

Musasir

NAIRI

Lake Van

Tushpa

ARME-SHUPRIA

r. Tigris

HAYASA

r. Euphrates

50 miles

100 km

Cimmerians and with the Scythians, new nomadic invaders who had penetrated the region from passes in the Caucasus. The Urartuan kings Argishti II (c. 714-685 B.C.) and Rusa II (c. 685-645 B.C.) paid tribute to Assyria and concentrated on repelling the nomads.

The last powerful Assyrian king was Ashur-banipal II (c. 668-624 B.C.) who tried to reclaim the greatness of Assyria by destroying the kingdom of Elam in western Persia, an action which allowed the rise of Elam's neighbor, Media. Simultaneously, a minor revival occurred in Urartu, and the great fortress of Teishebaini (in Armenian, Karmir Blur) was built on a hill north of Erebuni by Rusa II to store the royal treasury and to serve as a safe haven from the Scythians.

The history of the remaining half century of the Urartian kingdom is unclear. A number of kings ruled amidst internal and external conflicts. Among them was King Erimena, who may have been an Armenian. Erimena may have clashed with the established hierarchy, an action which, combined with renewed Scythian attacks, must have considerably weakened the kingdom. At the same time, the decline of both Urartu and Assyria, enabled the Medes to emerge as a new force. Around 670 B.C. they built their capital at Ecbatana and occupied parts of Persia. The Medes, together with Babylon and Egypt, combined forces to end the Assyrian hegemony in Mesopotamia. In 612 B.C. they sacked Nineveh, the Assyrian capital, and by 610 B.C. the Assyrian empire ceased to exist.

Unlike Assyria, which was relatively intolerant and depended solely on its military might, Urartu borrowed from other cultures and engaged in trade and diplomacy. Assyria prided itself on its centralized bureaucracy, but once that center was sacked, the Assyrian empire disintegrated. The Urartian confederation, a largely decentralized and tolerant state, however, managed to survive. These characteristics were adopted by the new leaders of the confederation, the Armenians.

The Medes and the Babylonians divided the Assyrian empire and its satellite states. The Babylonians formed the New Babylonian kingdom by taking the lands west of the Tigris River, all the way to the Mediterranean Sea. The Medes expanded to the regions east of the Tigris and invaded Urartu. They seem either to have subjugated members of the former confederation, or to have made tribute arrangements with the dominant group, which was probably the Armenian. In any case, somewhere between 605 and 585 B.C. the confederation became part of the Median empire.

Urartian Culture

During their three centuries of existence the Urartians built canals, palaces, cities and fortresses, some of which have been excavated in modern times. In addition, they created metal tools, weapons, jewelry, and pottery, fragments of which have been preserved and are on display in the museums of Armenia and in the Hermitage Museum in St. Petersburg, Russia. The Urartian pantheon included indigenous, Indo-European, and Assyrian gods. *Khaldi* was the main god and god of war; *Teishebaini* was the god of thunder; and *Shivini* represented the sun god. Horses were an important commodity both in the economy and the military, and the image of the horse was represented on Urartian shields. Assyrian and Etruscan influences can be found in Urartian art, demonstrating the extent of trade in the ancient world. Urartian bronzes and iron-works such as cauldrons, candelabra, and decorative shields were prized and have been found throughout the Transcaucasian and Greek worlds. Although at first much was copied from Assyria and the Hittites, a distinctive Urartian style soon emerged, a synthesis of many other art forms, which can be seen in the palace wall decorations at the Erebuni complex in Yerevan. Urartian inscriptions in Vannic cuneiform replaced Assyrian cuneiform. This wedge-shaped script had more than five hundred forms, many of which had multiple meanings. Trade and war had made Urartu wealthy, for the records describe the great riches taken by the Scythians and Assyrians in their campaigns against Urartu.

More than a thousand years later, when Armenian historians began to record the history of their nation, the existence of Urartu was unknown to them. The great Armenian historian Movses Khorenatsi (Moses of Khoren), making use of the oral tradition and written sources available to him, had transformed Arame, the first ruler of Urartu into the legendary Armenian king, *Ara the Handsome*. The Assyrians were personified by the evil, yet enticing, Queen *Semiramis* (Shammur-amat c. 810-805 B.C.), who lusted after Ara and caused his death. Although Arame and

Shammur-amat were not contemporaries, the struggle between their two states was symbolized in the narrative of Moses of Khoren. Ironically, the cuneiform fragments recording the greatness of the Urartuan kingdom stood mute before their historical descendants, who could no longer interpret them. Urartu, like most ancient civilizations, disappeared under the layers of classical and medieval civilizations, to be re-discovered only in the nineteenth and twentieth centuries.

III

From the Ark to Archeology:
The Origins of the Armenian People

As with many ancient peoples, the origins of the Armenians contain elements of myth and unresolved scholarly arguments. The explanations can be grouped into three versions: The Greek, the Armenian, and recent scholarly versions.

The Greek Versions

Greek legend has it that Armenia was named either after or by Armenus, one of Jason's argonauts. This myth, formulated after the Greeks colonized the Black Sea coast and parts of Asia Minor, served the purpose of stamping a Greek identity on all the peoples of the region. Ancient Greek historians, all writing long after the appearance of the Armenians, but well before the written works of Armenian chroniclers, have left a number of historical explanations as to the origins of the Armenian people. Two of the most quoted versions are by Herodotus and Strabo. According to the fifth-century B.C. historian, Herodotus, the Armenians had originally lived in Thrace from where they crossed into Phrygia in Asia Minor and had then gradually moved east of the Euphrates river to what became Armenia. According to the historian and geographer Strabo, who wrote in the first century B.C., Armenians came from two directions, one group from the west, or Phrygia, and the other from the southeast, or the Mesopotamian and Zagros region. In other words, according to the ancient Greeks, the Armenians were not the original

inhabitants of the region. They appear to have arrived sometime between
the Phrygian migration to Asia Minor in the thirteenth century B.C. and
the Cimmerian invasion of Urartu in the eight century B.C. The decline
of Urartu allowed the Armenians to establish themselves as the primary
occupants of the region. Xenophon, who, as will be discussed in chapter
IV, passed through Armenia in 400 B.C., recorded that, by his time, the
Armenians had absorbed most of the local inhabitants.

The Armenian Versions

According to the earliest Armenian accounts, written sometime between
the fifth and eight centuries A.D., the Armenian people are the descendants of Japheth, a son of Noah. After the ark had landed on Mt. Ararat,
Noah's family settled first in Armenia and, generations later, moved
south to the land of Babylon. The leader of the Armenians, Haik, a
descendant of Japheth, unhappy with the tyranny and evil in Babylon,
rebelled and decided to return to the land of the ark. The evil Bel, leader
of the Babylonians, pursued Haik. In the ensuing war, good conquered
evil when Haik killed Bel and created an Armenian nation. Haik became
the first Armenian ruler and his sons continued to lead the Armenians
until King Paruir, a descendent of Haik, formed the first kingdom of
Armenia and had to face the mighty Assyrian foe.

This legend, probably as old as Mesopotamian legends, including that
of Gilgamesh, not only blends historical facts with fable but manages to
place the Armenians in a prominent position within the biblical tradition.
Noah, after all, was "the second Adam," his descendants chosen and
blessed by God to repopulate the earth. Armenians, like the Jews, thus
had a special calling to fight the evil Babylonians and to live in accordance
to the laws of God. The periodic floods in Mesopotamia must have left
vivid memories for the people living in Western Asia. Numerous invasions into the region, particularly that of Assyria, and Assyria's clashes
with pre-Armenian rulers, had been etched into the folklore of the local
Caucasian and Indo-European inhabitants. It is not surprising, therefore,
that between 440 and 840 A.D. early Armenian historians, such as Moses
of Khoren, who did not have our historical and archeological data,
recorded the oral tradition by substituting Babylon for Assyria and the

Haik family for the Urartian rulers in Armenia. The aim was not accuracy but rather a sure place for the Armenians in the history of Christianity, a religion the Armenians had by then embraced enthusiastically.

Recent Scholarly Versions

Modern archeological finds have presented a more detailed, although not complete, version of the possible origins of the Armenians. Until a few decades ago, scholars maintained that the Armenians were an Indo-European group who either came into the area with the Mitanni from the Aral Sea region or arrived from the Balkans with the Phrygians. It was believed that they either became part of the Urartian confederation or were concentrated around the Euphrates until the Cimmero-Scythian invasions altered the power structure in the region. The Armenians then managed to consolidate their rule over Urartu and, in time, assimilated most of its Caucasian and Indo-European groups to form the Armenian nation.

More recent scholarship offers yet another possibility, that the Armenians were not later immigrants, but were part of the original inhabitants of the region. Although this notion has gained credibility, there remain a number of unresolved questions: What was the spoken language of the early Armenians? Did the Indo-European proto-language originate in Transcaucasia or in Europe? In other words, are the Armenians members of a non Indo-European, Caucasian-speaking group, who later adopted an Indo-European dialect, or are they one of the native Indo-European-speaking groups?

A number of linguists maintain that two Armenian tribes, the Hayasa and the Urm or Arm, together with the Hurrian, Guti, Kassites and others, were Caucasian tribes who lived in the region until the arrival of the Indo-Europeans. The Armenians adopted part of their later language from these Indo-European arrivals. This explains why Armenian is a unique branch of the Indo-European language tree and may well explain the origin of the words *Hai* and *Hayastan* ("Armenian" and "Armenia" in the Armenian language), as well as the word *Armenian*. As evidence, these scholars point to Hurrian suffixes, the absence of gender, and other linguistic and archeological data, such as the images of Armenians on a

number of sixth-century Persian monuments which depict racial characteristics similar to those of other people of the Caucasus.

Other scholars, also relying on linguistic evidence, believe that Indo-
European languages originated in Transcaucasia and that the Armenians,
as a result of pressure from large empires such as the Hittite and Assyrian,
merged with neighboring tribes, adopted a number of Semitic and
Kartvelian words, and consolidated themselves into federations such as
Nairi, Hayasa-Azzi, and Arme-Shupria and, eventually, into the united
kingdom of Urartu. The decline and fall of Urartu allowed the Armenian
component to achieve predominance and by the sixth century B.C.,
establish a separate entity, which the Greeks and Persians, the new major
powers of the ancient world, called Armenia.

B.C.E.	ARMENIA	MIDDLE EAST, PERSIA & EGYPT	GREECE & ROME	INDIA, CHINA & JAPAN	SUB-SAHARAN AFRICA & THE AMERICAS
600	Medes conquer Urartu Yervandunis vassals of Medes (c. 570-550) Yervandunis vassals of Persia (c. 550-530) Revolts in Armenia, Armeno-Persian satraps (c. 530-410)	Kush rule in Egypt Lydians invent coins (c. 600) Height of Median empire (c. 580-550) Babylonian captivity of Jews (586-538) Nebuchadnezzar builds the Hanging Gardens of Babylon, one of the Seven Wonders of the ancient world Persian Achaemenid empire (550-331) End of Babylonian captivity, rebuilding of Temple in Jerusalem (538) Persian conquest of Egypt (525) Darius I (522-486) Behistun monument (c. 520) Royal road built	Solon's reforms in Athens (594) Pythagoras (c. 582-507) Aeschylus (c. 525-456) Roman republic founded (509) Athenian democracy begins (508)	Chou Dynasty to 256 Buddha (c. 563-483) Confucius (c. 551-479) Lao-Tzu (c. 550) Mahavira, founder of Jainism (c. 540-468)	Olmec civilization in La Vente to 400
500		Xerxes I (486-465)	Ionic architectural style in Greece (c. 500-400) Phidias (c. 500-432) Orphic and Eleusinian cults (c. 500-100) Sophocles (c. 496-406) Greco-Persian wars (499-478) Pericles (494-429) Herodotus (c. 484-424) Euripides (c. 480-406) Delian League (479-404) Socrates (c. 469-399) Thucydides (460-400) Hippocrates (c. 460-377) Parthenon (c. 450) Alcibaides (c. 450-404) Aristophanes (c. 445-385) Peloponnesian War (431-404) Plato (c. 426-347)	Use of iron in China (c. 500) Cross-bow and metal tools in China (450)	Nok culture in Africa (c. 500)
400	Yervandunis re-appear as satraps (c. 410)				

Table 3: 600 B.C. to 200 B.C.

B.C.E.	ARMENIA	MIDDLE EAST, PERSIA & EGYPT	GREECE & ROME	INDIA, CHINA & JAPAN	SUB-SAHARAN AFRICA & THE AMERICAS
400	Xenophon in Armenia (401-400) Armenia autonomous (c. 330-300)	Battle of Issus (333) Battle of Gaugamela, end of Persian empire (331) Death of Alexander the Great (323) Seleucid dynasty begins (c. 312)	Corinthian architectural style in Greece (c. 400-300) Aristotle (c. 384-322) Epicurus (c. 342-270) Zeno the Stoic (c. 320-250) Euclid (c. 320-285) Death of Demosthenes (322)	Use of coins in China Indian epics (400-200 A.D.) Magadha Kingdom Nanda dynasty in India Chandragupta and the Mauryan empire (322-185) Rise of Taoism in China The Mahabharata	
300	Greater Armenia ruled by Yervandunis as an independent state (c. 300-200)	Seleucus I (305-281) Ptolemy dynasty in Egypt	Archimedes (c. 287-212) Punic wars between Rome and Carthage (264-146) Rome advances into Greece (215) Polybius (205-118)	The Ramayana Ashoka (c. 270-232) Bhagavad Gita Fall of the Chou dynasty (256) Legalism in China (c. 250) Ch'in dynasty (221-207) Great Wall (c. 220-207) Tomb of First Emperor in Xian (c. 210-200) Han Dynasty (202-220 A.D.) in China I Ching in China	Olmec civilization in Tres Zapotes Early calendars in America
200	End of Yervanduni rule (c. 200)				

Table 3: 600 B.C. to 200 B.C.

IV

From Satraps To Kings:

The Yervandunis (Orontids), the First Armenian Dynasty (c. 585-200 B.C.)

The four centuries between the end of the Urartuan kingdom and the beginning of the Armenian kingdom under the Artashesian (Artaxiad) dynasty were formative years not only for the Armenians but for most of the peoples and cultures of the time. Many of today's religions, languages, arts, philosophies, and legal systems evolved during this period. It saw the dominance of the Indo-Europeans and the flowering of the Classical Age in Eurasia.

In the Middle East, the empire of the Medes was replaced by the first great Persian or Iranian empire, which for the next two centuries controlled much of that region, as well as Central Asia and Egypt. In Europe, Classical Greece witnessed its golden age and the rise of city states, as well as their decline and eventual conquest by Philip of Macedon. Alexander the Great conquered a large part of the civilized world, defeated the Persian empire, and introduced Hellenism into Asia and north Africa. Rome founded its republic, consolidated its power on the Italian peninsula, defeated Carthage, absorbed the Greece of Alexander's successors, and challenged their power in Asia and Africa. The Mauryan empire united India, and Buddhism, Jainism, and Hinduism, spread throughout South Asia. In East Asia, during the Chou, Ch'in, and the first period of the Han dynasties, China began its unification within the Great Wall, under the philosophical and social guidance of Confucianism, Taoism,

Legalism, and the I Ching. The Olmec culture continued to flourish in
Mexico, while in sub-Saharan Africa, city states began to emerge.

Until a few decades ago, it was thought that the first Armenian dynasty
appeared only at the beginning of the second century B.C. There is new
evidence, however, of an earlier family, the Yervandunis (Orontids), who
ruled in Armenia as governors appointed by the Medes and Persians and,
after the fall of the Persian empire to Alexander the Great, ruled independently. Although some believe the Yervandunis were of Urartian
origin, the background of the Yervandunis is unknown, beyond the fact
that they were probably linked, by blood or marriage, to the Persian royal
family. It is possible, however, that, if not Armenian themselves, the
Yervandunis eventually intermarried with Armenians. The term
Yervanduni is derived from *Yervand*, the name of at least four of the
dynasty's leaders. Not much else is known about the Yervandunis.
Successive dynasties and invasions have obliterated most of the culture
of Armenia in this period. However, in Nimrud-dagh, Turkey, a com-
memorative monument of the first century B.C., erected by a ruler of
Commagene, who was related to the Yervandunis, mentions a number
of his Yervanduni ancestors who had ruled Armenia.

The Medes and Armenia

As described previously, the Medes, together with the Babylonians, had
crushed and divided much of the Assyrian empire by 610 B.C. The New
Babylonian kingdom lasted less than a century. Its most famous ruler
was Nebuchednezzar, who conquered Jerusalem and took many Jews
as slaves, thus beginning their Babylonian captivity. The Medes, in the
meanwhile, went on to annex parts of Urartu and Mesopotamia and, by
585 B.C., had become a major power. The Medes appointed local
governors to maintain control over their large territory, which included
Elam, Cappadocia, Parthia, and Persia, as well as Urartu/Armenia. A
Yervanduni family member administered this last province.

The Persian Empire and the Armenians

By the mid-sixth century B.C., a number of these vassal groups, the

Yervandunis among them, had rebelled against the Medes, under the leadership of Cyrus of Persia. By 550 B.C. Cyrus had overthrown the Medes and founded the Achaemenid dynasty. Cyrus and his son, Cambyses, then conquered a territory stretching from India to the Aegean and Mediterranean Seas, including Armenia, and Egypt. In the process they freed the Jews from their Babylonian captivity and permitted the reconstruction of the temple of Jerusalem. It was Darius I, another member of the Achaemenid family, however, who forged this multi-national territory into the great Persian empire which lasted until its defeat by Alexander the Great in 331 B.C.

Little is known about the Armenians during this period, though they probably still shared land and military power with the other groups inhabiting the former Urartuan state. Tradition has it that while hostage at the Median court, Cyrus befriended another hostage, the Armenian prince, Tigran-Yervand, and thus established good relations between the Armenians and the Persians, which later enabled the Armenians to control all of the former Urartuan state. In fact, by the late sixth century B.C., Armenian power and cultural dominance must have increased significantly, for after only three generations following the fall of Urartu, the Armenians were sufficiently important to be included among the major provinces or *satrapies* and peoples listed on the Behistun (Bisotun) rock, erected by Darius I in 520/519 B.C. to commemorate his achievements and conquests. This is the first time that the name *Armenia* and *Armenian* (inscribed as *Armina* and *Arminiya*) appear in recorded history. Although the Armenians refer to themselves as *Hai*, the Persian and Greek (the latter referring to Armenians as *Armenioi*) terms were adopted by non Armenians.

Darius organized his empire into twenty *satrapies* and placed trusted family members or friends as *satraps* or governors of these provinces (see map 4). Although it was once believed that Armenia was included in the 13th and 18th *satrapies*, evidence now suggests that it probably lay either in the 10th or the 13th province. Darius conducted a number of campaigns against the Armenians, who had rebelled against his new taxes. He may have appointed a Persian or another Armenian family as *satraps* rather than the Yervandunis, for there is no mention of them as provincial governors until the next century.

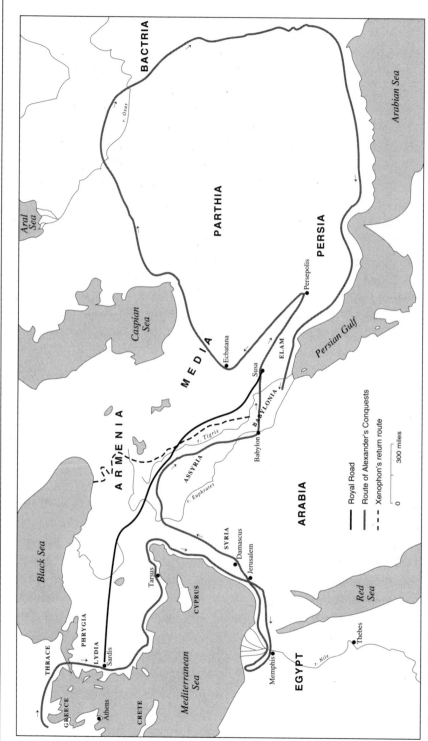

4. The Persian Empire (c. 500–330 B.C.)

The empire was soon connected by a royal road which linked Susa in central Persia with Sardis in western Asia Minor. The road had rest stops for royal messengers and travellers; fifteen of these stations stretching some 150 miles, passed through southern Armenia (see map 4). Although the Armenians had to pay a large annual tribute in silver and horses, as well as contribute contingents to the Persian army, their inclusion in the empire and the communications made possible by the royal road, enabled the Armenians to gradually consolidate much of the former Urartuan lands into a single cultural unit. The Achaemenids were tolerant, and as long as peace was maintained and tribute paid, they allowed their subject peoples, including the Armenians, to follow local customs and worship their own deities. From the late sixth century B.C. onward, Armenia was left to its *satraps* and generally existed peacefully within the Persian empire until the end of the Achaemenid dynasty. Armenians served in the Persian army in the Greek and other campaigns during the 5th and 4th centuries B.C. and were among the Persian forces of Darius III defending Persia against Alexander the Great.

The main source on Armenia in this period is the *Anabasis* by the Greek historian Xenophon, an eyewitness to the events in the region in 401-400 B.C. Xenophon was among the Greek troops who had entered Persia to intervene on behalf of a candidate in a disputed succession. Unfortunately for the Greeks, their candidate was defeated prior to their arrival and they were forced to retreat through Armenia (see map 4). Xenophon mentioned a Yervand, the son-in-law of the Persian king Artaxerxes I, ruling in the eastern parts of Armenia. He recorded that the *satrapy* had an Armenian as well as a non-Armenian population, which remained isolated in the highlands. These last were probably some of the Urartuans who had resisted assimilation. Some historians claim that they are the ancestors of the present-day Kurds. (Other historians maintain that the Kurds are the descendants of the ancient Medes). Xenophon also mentioned Tiribazus, the governor of the western parts of Armenia and a personal friend of the Persian king, who alone had the honor of assisting the king in mounting his horse. In Xenophon's description of the land itself, he did not mention the existence of any major cities, but recorded that the region was made up of villages with fortified houses above ground, as well as underground winter quarters. Armenian was spoken by a large portion of the population, while the people of the hills had their own dialect. The *satrap* worked with the clan elders, who mediated between the people and the provincial administration. The population was mainly engaged in agriculture and raising livestock, including the famed Armenian horses, thousands of which were sent as annual tribute to Persia. Xenophon reported that there was plenty of food, including a variety of meats, vegetables, breads, oils, and wines. He also described a kind of beer drunk with what resembled a straw, one of the early mention of these in recorded history. Armenians are depicted as short and stocky with straight dark hair, dark eyes, and prominent noses. In a relief at Persepolis the Armenians are depicted presenting a horse and other tribute. They are dressed much like the Medes of that time, with long hair tied at the back of their necks, and with tunics down to the knees, worn over pants tied at the ankles. Aramaic, the language of the imperial administration, was introduced into Armenia, where, for centuries, it continued to be used in official documents. Old Persian cuneiform, meanwhile, was used in most inscriptions.

Xenophon used a Persian interpreter to converse with Armenians and in some of the Armenian villages they responded in Persian, evidence that knowledge of Persian had spread among the Armenians. The influence of Persia on the Armenian language is evident from the many Iranian words which remain in the Armenian language until today. The Armenians adapted the Persian social structure and the Zoroastrian pantheon, which included *Aramazd*, the creator of heaven and earth; *Mihr*, the god of light; *Astghik*, the goddess of love; *Vahagn*, the god of war; *Tir*, the god of the arts and sciences; and *Anahit*, the goddess of fertility and wisdom. The cult of *Mithra*, as well as other cults and religious beliefs which were prevalent in the Persian empire, slowly made inroads in Armenia. The many temples of *Anahit* in Armenia and festivals dedicated to her indicate that this Zoroastrian goddess had become a particular favorite among the Armenians and that she served as their protector. Despite the degree of Median and Persian influence, however, an Armenian identity, influenced by local traditions, gradually took shape.

With the decline of the Achaemenids, some of the *satrapies* began to assert their autonomy. By the mid-fourth century B.C., the Yervandunis had united much of Armenia into a single province, established marriage alliances with their western neighbor, Commagene, and had, in effect, created an autonomous unit within the Persian empire.

Alexander the Great and Hellenism

During these two centuries, the Persians repeatedly tried to control the Greek mainland, a struggle which Herodotus has recorded in his history of the Greco-Persian Wars. Although never successful, Persia threatened Greece by supplying contending Greek city states with gold. This threat was eliminated when Alexander the Great crossed into Asia and attacked the Persian empire. Darius III, the last of the Achaemenids, together with his vassals, including the Armenian *satrap*, another Yervand, tried to defend his empire, but was crushed in the battles of Issus in 333 B.C. and Gaugamela in 331 B.C. According to later Roman historians, the Armenian contingent in these battles was very large. In conquering a good part of the civilized world, Alexander founded new cities and military colonies, and settled Greeks and Macedonians throughout Asia and North Africa (see map 4). Greek culture mixed with that of the indigenous Eastern peoples and a Hellenistic culture emerged.

The Seleucids (312-64 B.C.)

Following the death of Alexander the Great in 323 B.C., his Asian and African conquests were soon divided between two of his generals. Seleucus claimed the former Persian empire and founded the Seleucid dynasty, while Ptolemy took over Egypt and founded the Ptolemaic dynasty (see map 5). While the early Seleucids brought with them the Greek concept of oligarchical city states, these Western ideas were not readily accepted in every part of the former Persian empire. As Greek culture was essentially an urban one, the Seleucids had to establish new cities in order to attract Greek settlers and administrators. Division and discrimination began to occur between Greeks and non-Greeks. The Seleucids eventually adopted the Persian concept of kingship, while retaining a mostly Hellenistic religion and culture.

Early in their reign, the Seleucids gave up their Indian holdings to Chandragupta Maurya in exchange for 500 elephants to use against their

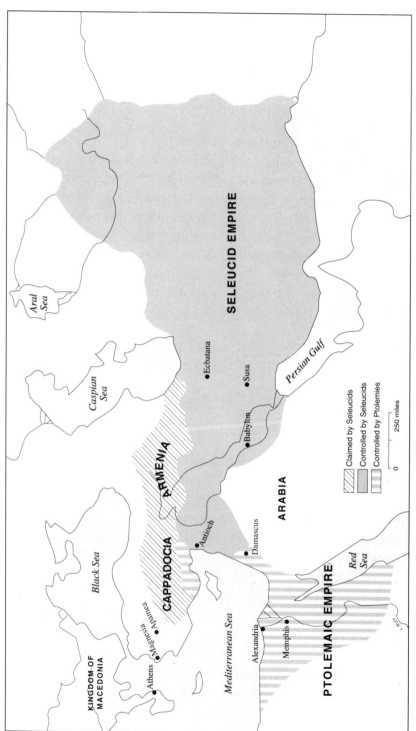

5. The Hellenistic Empires (c. 300 B.C.)

SELEUCID EMPIRE

Aral
Sea

Caspian
Sea

• Ecbatana

• Susa

Persian Gulf

• Babylon

ARMENIA

CAPPADOCIA

Antioch •

• Damascus

ARABIA

Black Sea

• Apamea
Magnesia •

Athens •

KINGDOM· OF
MACEDONIA

Mediterranean Sea

Red
Sea

PTOLEMAIC EMPIRE

Alexandria •
• Memphis

Claimed by Seleucids

Controlled by Seleucids

Controlled by Ptolemies

0   250 miles

enemies. Fifty years later the Seleucid empire was reduced further when eastern Persia declared its independence under the Parthians and Central Asia broke away under a Greco-Bactrian dynasty.

Independent Yervanduni Rule in Armenia

Meanwhile, the collapse of the Achaemenid empire had created an opportunity for the Yervandunis to assert complete independence. Since Alexander had never passed through Armenia, and, therefore, left no military presence in the region, the Yervandunis were able to refuse tribute to and revolt against Alexander's appointed governors. After the death of Alexander, the Armenians maintained this stance towards the Seleucids as well. The Yervandunis gained control of the Arax valley, reached Lake Sevan, and constructed a new capital at Yervandashat, at the confluence of the Arax and Akhurian rivers, to replace Armavir, which had been vulnerable to Seleucid attacks. According to tradition they also built a new religious center at Bagaran, north of Yervandashat, on the left bank of the Akhurian. Although the Yervandunis ruled much of Armenia, they were never able to control the more Hellenistic western regions. By the third century B.C. three Armenias had emerged: Lesser Armenia or Armenia Minor, northwest of the Euphrates; Greater Armenia or Armenian Major; and Sophene or Dsopk, in the southwest (see map 6). Lesser Armenia came under Hellenistic influence and occasionally under the political control of either the Seleucids, the rulers of Pontus, or Cappadocia. Greater Armenia, encompassing most of historic Armenia, maintained much of its political autonomy due to its relative geographical isolation, the wars between the Seleucids and their rivals, and the removal of the Seleucid seat of government to Antioch in distant Syria. Dsopk, located along the royal road, was at different times, depending on political circumstances, either independent or part of Greater Armenia. The Yervandunis continued to govern Greater Armenia and Dsopk, and although a number of Seleucid kings, among them Seleucus I, tried to subdue these areas, they soon accepted the independent status of the Yervandunis.

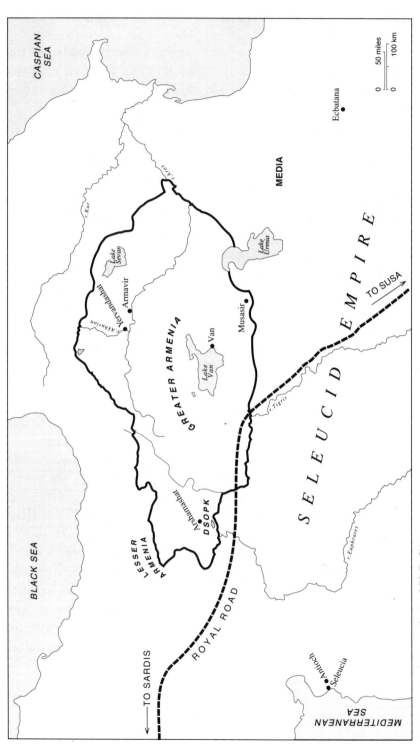

6. Yervanduni Armenia (c. 250 B.C.)

Society and Culture

During the two centuries of Seleucid presence, Greek, now the language of commerce and the arts in the Middle East, periodically replaced Aramaic as the administrative language of Armenia and was frequently spoken by the upper classes. In Armenia, Greek-style temples to Apollo and Artemis were built. Coins with Greek inscription appeared there, as they did all over Asia. International commerce passed through Armenia, bringing with it both Eastern and Western culture and science. Although the Greek calendar, law, and religious beliefs, as well as theater, philosophy, art and architecture, now made inroads, Greater Armenia became only partially influenced by Hellenism. Persian (Iranian) culture, as well as the Armenian language and customs remained a dominant force. The most important change was the rise of cities, such as Yervandashat, Yervandakert, and Arshamashat (Arsamosata), which facilitated the unification of Greater Armenia. The Yervandunis must be judged as tenacious rulers. They resisted Darius I in a number of rebellions, achieved some degree of autonomy during the decline of the Persian empire, rejected Alexander's governors, rebuffed the Seleucids, and maintained their independence. Furthermore, despite adopting certain aspects of Hellenism, the Armenians under Yervanduni rule maintained their own culture and traditions.

Yervanduni dominance came to an end when the Seleucids, under Antiochus III (223-187 B.C.), attempted to revive their empire and to make Armenia a vassal state. An Armenian nobleman, Artashes (Artaxias), who was probably related to the Yervandunis, was encouraged by Antiochus to rebel, and around 200 B.C., together with another relative, overthrew the last Yervanduni, laying the foundations of the first Armenian kingdom.

B.C.E.	ARMENIA	MIDDLE EAST, PERSIA & EGYPT	GREECE & ROME	INDIA, CHINA & JAPAN	SUB-SAHARAN AFRICA & THE AMERICAS
200		Ptolemaic rule in Egypt continues Battle of Magnesia, Rome enters Asia (190) Mithradates I of Parthia (171-138) Jewish revolt led by Judas Maccabeus (167-165) End of Seleucid power in Syria (129)	Skeptics (c. 200-100) Rome annexes Greece and Macedon (148) Carthage destroyed (146) Stoicism in Rome (c. 140) Reform of the Gracchi (133-121) Cicero (106-43)	Han dynasty to 220 A.D. Bactrian Rule Hellenism in western India Silk road opens China to Parthia and Rome (c. 104)	Decline of Olmec civilization in Mexico Increase of food production in sub-Saharan Africa
	Artashes overthrows Yervanduni rule (c.200) Artashes I (189-160) Artashesian Dynasty (c. 189-10 A.D.) Artavazd I (160-115) Tigran I (115-95)				
100	Tigran II (95-55) Armenian Empire	Dead Sea Scrolls (c.100)	Lucretius (98-55) Roman citizenship granted to residents of Italy (90) Sulla in Greece (88-84) Sulla's dictatorship (88-79) Revolt of Spartacus (73-71) Virgil (70-19)	Yamato clan forms Japanese state (c. 100)	Early Teotihuacan culture in Mexico
	Lucullus invades Armenia (69-68)	Lucullus invades Asia Minor (73) Death of Mithradates of Pontus (65) Pompey declares Syria a Roman province (64)	Horace (65-8 A.D.) First Triumvirate (60-53) Livy (59-17 A.D.) Death of Crassus (53) Pompey's dictatorship (51-49)		
	Pompey invades Armenia (66) Artavazd II (55-35) Mark Antony invades Armenia (35) Artashes II (30-20) Decline and fall of the Artashesian dynasty	Battle of Carrhae (53) Kushans invade eastern Parthia Roman-Parthian conflict in Syria Death of Cleopatra, end of Ptolemaic rule, Egypt a Roman province (30)	Caesar crosses the Rubicon (49) Death of Pompey (48) Caesar's dictatorship (46-44) Death of Caesar (44) Second Triumvirate (43-36) Ovid (43-18 A.D.) Seneca (4 to 65 A. D.) Battle of Actium (31) Death of Antony (30) End of Roman Republic (27) Augustus (27 to 14 A.D.)	Kushans rule north-western India (c. 25-225 A.D.)	Early Mayan culture in Central America
C.E.	Roman-Parthian conflict in Armenia		Birth of Christ (c. 4 B.C.) Tiberius (14-37) Pliny the Elder (23-79) Crucifixion (30) St. Paul's missionary activity (35-67) Caligula (37-41) Claudius (41-54)		

Table 4: 200 B.C. to 50 A.D.

V

Between Roman Legions and Parthian Cavalry:

The Artashesian (Artaxiad) Dynasty and the Formation of the Armenian Kingdom (c. 189 B.C.-10 A.D.)

The last two centuries before the birth of Christ were a significant era in global civilization. The great Han Dynasty began its more than four hundred-year rule in China and the Yamato clan established the foundations of the first Japanese state. The Ptolemies continued to rule Egypt. Various invaders fragmented the Mauryan empire in India, and elements of Hellenism were introduced to its northwestern provinces. In Persia, the Parthians, who had emerged in the previous century, formed an empire under the Arsacid dynasty. The most important development in the West was the rise of the Roman republic, which annihilated the Carthaginians in Africa, conquered Greece and Macedonia, and replaced the Seleucid state in Syria and Asia Minor. The same period witnessed the birth of the first recognized Armenian kingdom and its new strategic importance to the powers which surrounded it.

The Yervandunis had, as previously noted, resisted Seleucid encroachments and kept Greater Armenia independent. The rise of Rome and its push into Greece and Macedonia, threatened the Seleucid position in Syria. Antiochus III, the last noteworthy ruler of the line, attempted to restore the Seleucid empire by halting the advance of the Parthians, who by the second century B.C. had gradually penetrated as far as central Persia. He then sought to extend his sovereignty over the autonomous regions bordering his domains. At the start of the second century B.C., Antiochus succeeded in persuading some members of the Yervanduni family to challenge their head and to switch their allegiance to the Seleucids. Artashes and Zareh (Zariadres) accepted his offer, rebelled against the last Yervanduni, received military titles from Antiochus, and established themselves as governors of Armenia. Artashes took control of Yervandashat and all the territory of Greater Armenia, while Zareh took Dsopk.

Roman Presence in the East

Feeling secure in the east, Antiochus envisioned a new Hellenistic empire, under the leadership of the Seleucids. He consequently advanced into Macedonia and Greece and attempted to dislodge Roman presence there and to expand Seleucid control over the land of Alexander the Great. In 190 B.C., however, he was defeated by Rome in the battle of Magnesia, and by the Peace of Apamea (188 B.C.), lost his possessions in Asia Minor and northwestern Syria. Rome's foothold in Asia was now secure, a fact which was to affect the region for the next eight centuries. The Seleucid kingdom, on the other hand, was now squeezed into Syria and Palestine, where it encountered new problems. When Antiochus IV, known as Epiphanes, desecrated the Temple of Jerusalem, the Jews, under the leadership of Judas Maccabeus, revolted in 168 B.C., a conflict which preoccupied the Seleucids for the next three years. Taking advantage of this situation, the Parthians took control of Persia and became a new power in the East. Rome fashioned a strategy to further weaken the Seleucids and at the same time protect its own holdings by encouraging the fragmentation of the former Seleucid empire in Asia Minor into smaller states, friendly to Rome, which would act as a buffer against any future Parthian advances west of Mesopotamia. Armenia, Cappadocia, Commagene, and Pontus thus emerged as Roman allies, and, after Magnesia, were formally recognized by Rome as independent kingdoms.

Artashes and the Foundation of a New Dynasty

Artashes, who claimed relationship to both the Yervanduni and Persian noble houses, was recognized by Rome as the king of Armenia in 189 or 188 B.C. Armenia was now regarded as a sovereign state by both Parthia and Rome. Artashes initiated his rule by conducting a survey of his land. His boundary stones, the first ever recorded in Armenia, written in Aramaic, have been found in the area of Lake Sevan. To confirm the new status of his country and to break from the Yervanduni past, Artashes built a new capital city, Artashat (Artaxata), on the left bank of the Arax River near present-day Khorvirap. This well-planned Hellenistic city remained the capital of Armenia for the next four hundred years. Statues of various Greek and Persian divinities were brought by Artashes to the new city from the Yervanduni religious center at Bagaran, making Artashat both the political and religious center of the new Armenian kingdom. The size of the city and its great fortifications gave rise to the legend that Hannibal of Carthage had helped in its planning and construction. Although both Strabo and Plutarch reiterate this claim, there is no evidence to substantiate it. Artashes established an administrative structure and a tax system, and distributed land among his family and faithful retainers. Moreover, he expanded his territory by annexing regions inhabited by the Medes, Caucasian Albanians, and the Iberians (Georgians). His efforts to conquer Dsopk from Zareh, however, proved unsuccessful. Lesser Armenia, under the control of Pontus, also remained outside the Artashesian domains (see map 7).

The Seleucids, who were trying to regain control of the Syrian coast and Mesopotamia, finally subdued the Jews in 165 B.C. and attacked both Parthia and Armenia at the end of Artsahes' reign. Artashes was defeated and captured by Antiochus IV but continued to rule in exchange for tribute. Rome, which viewed Armenia and its fellow buffer states as allies or, more probably, potential vassals, was unhappy with the situation in Armenia, but its own domestic problems and its final campaign in Carthage left it too preoccupied to intervene in the affairs of Asia. The Seleucids, in the long run, did not manage to restore their dominance and for the next hundred years ruled only in parts of Syria. The Parthians, however, filled the power vacuum handily and, under the leadership of Mithradates I (171-138 B.C.), who was an Arsacid, became a major force, adopting both the Persian and Hellenistic culture of their predecessors. They soon established themselves in Mesopotamia and built another

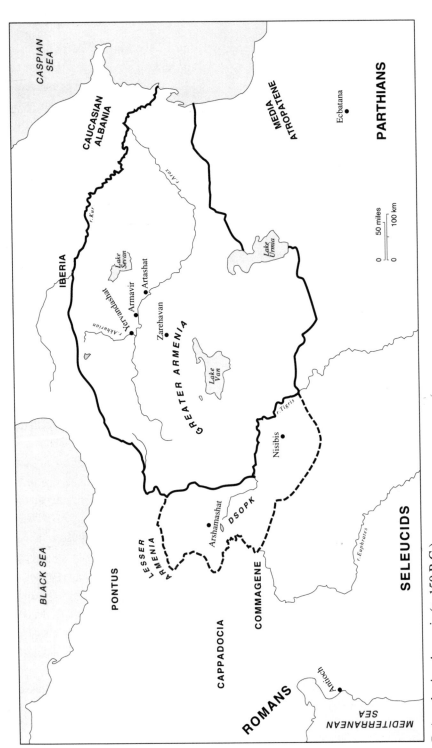

CASPIAN SEA

CAUCASIAN ALBANIA

MEDIA ATROPATENE

Ecbatana

PARTHIANS

r. Araxes

IBERIA

r. Kur

Lake Sevan

Lake Urmia

Artashat

Armavir

r. Akhurian

Yerandashat

Zarehavan

GREATER ARMENIA

Lake Van

r. Tigris

Nisibis

50 miles
0
100 km
0

BLACK SEA

PONTUS

LESSER ARMENIA

Arshamashat

DSOPK

COMMAGENE

CAPPADOCIA

r. Euphrates

SELEUCIDS

Antioch

MEDITERRANEAN SEA

ROMANS

7. Artashesian Armenia (c. 150 B.C.)

capital at Ctesiphon on the Tigris river. Rome, in the meantime, was content to consolidate its position in Asia Minor and gradually extend its influence to the Euphrates river. It was just a matter of time, therefore, before the two new powers would be embroiled in a rivalry which would continue for more than three centuries.

For the moment, Rome's lack of involvement left the successors of Artashes, Artavazd I (160-115 B.C.) and Tigran (Tigranes) I (115-95 B.C.) subject to the whims of the Parthians. Artavazd was defeated by the Parthians and had to send his nephew as hostage to Ctesiphon. For the rest of that century, as long as Armenia paid tribute and submitted hostages, relations with Parthia were peaceful. This peace was fostered by trade among China, Rome, and Parthia, made possible by the accessibility to the silk road in the first century B.C. The Parthians realized the importance of Armenia as a major trade emporium, and Artashat became an important stopover for this East-West commerce. The Artashesians established a mint in Armenia to further facilitate trade. Trade and the rise of new cities, further invited Hellenistic influences. At the same time Dsopk's expansion to the south and west, helped to bring the two Armenias closer together culturally. Greek and Persian remained the languages of the Armenian upper classes, while the masses in both Armenias spoke Armenian. Aramaic, with many Persian terms, continued to be the language of administration.

The last century of the pre-Christian era was dominated by power struggles between Rome and Parthia, with both trying to gain control of the fragmented Seleucid territories, as well as Armenia. After destroying Carthage and carrying out a number of domestic reforms, Rome finally set its eyes, once again, on Asia. Roman legions arrived in Syria and forced the local rulers to accept Roman authority. Seeking to secure Asia Minor, Rome gained control of Cappadocia and Commagene. In 96 B.C. Sulla, the Roman governor of Cilicia, and the representatives of Parthia met to partition the disputed territories into zones of influence. Roman actions in Asia, however, antagonized the leader of the Pontic kingdom, Mithradates VI Eupator, a Hellenistic nobleman of Persian descent, who wished to revive the Empire of the Seleucids, and he soon embarked on a mission to liberate Asia Minor and Greece from the Romans.

Meanwhile, the situation in Rome was far from stable. The social reforms of the Gracchi brothers had not been fully implemented, and the Italians had revolted over the issue of full citizenship. Having conquered a large territory in a short time, Rome was unprepared to administer it. The military and the Senate were vying for power. Republican rule was tested repeatedly as generals, particularly those who had achieved fame and fortune in foreign campaigns, tried to assume control over the state.

Tigran the Great

Following the death of Tigran I of Armenia in 95 B.C., his son Tigran II, a hostage at Ctesiphon, agreed to cede to Parthia a number of valleys in southeastern Armenia in return for his freedom. Tigran's first act after taking power at home was to conquer Dsopk and unite the two Armenias politically. Thereafter, except for short intervals, Dsopk remained part of Greater Armenia. Lesser Armenia, however, continued to remain outside the Armenian kingdom and, in fact, would never be under the same ruler as Greater Armenia. Tigran and Mithradates of Pontus realized that Roman and Parthian presence in the region was a constant danger to their own sovereignty. Civil war in Rome and problems over the succession in Parthia, encouraged them to attempt the creation of a third force in the region, a federation led by Pontus and Armenia, which would challenge Parthia and Rome. The alliance was sealed by the marriage of Tigran to the daughter of Mithradates. His eastern flank secure, Mithradates annexed Cappadocia and the coast of Asia Minor. Parthia and Rome, realizing that this alliance would be detrimental to their own designs, agreed to forgo their differences and to concentrate on eliminating the new threat. This was the first but not the last time that the two powers would divide the region into zones of influence. Sulla, who like subsequent Roman commanders viewed a successful eastern campaign as an opportunity to gain politically and materially, returned to drive the Pontic ruler out of Cappadocia. In 84 B.C. he managed to force Mithradates out of Greece and returned to Rome to assume the title of dictator. Mithradates did not give up his quest, however, and for the next ten years kept the Romans occupied by invading Greece and challenging Roman authority in Asia Minor.

With Mithradates keeping the Romans at bay and the western flank secure, Tigran concentrated on the east. The death of the Parthian king and nomadic invasions of Parthia from Central Asia, allowed Tigran in 90 B.C. to retake the valleys he had ceded to Parthia; he then expanded south and took parts of Mesopotamia. By 85 B.C. Tigran began using the Persian title "King of Kings" and had four viceroys in official attendance. When a group of Syrian nobles invited Tigran to rule, he annexed Commagene, northern Syria, Cilicia and Phoenicia. Tigran's empire thus extended from the Mediterranean to the Caspian Sea, and for a brief period, Armenia was an empire. (See map 8.) Antioch, the great Seleucid city and the capital of Syria, became Tigran's headquarters in the Levant. Tigran thus took control of much of the former Seleucid territory east of the Euphrates. To better manage his large empire, however, Tigran built a new capital, Tigranakert (Tigranocerta), and forced immigration of Jews, Arabs, and Greeks from Mesopotamia, Cilicia, and Cappadocia in order to populate it and other new Armenian cities. Tigranakert was a great city with walls reportedly so wide that store houses and stables could be built inside them. A theater was built in which Greek plays were performed. Parks and hunting grounds surrounded the city. Unfortunately, the remains of Tigranakert have not been found and its site has been debated, although it probably lay somewhere between Tell Ermen, Amida (present-day Diyarbekir), and Martyropolis (present-day Miyafarkin). With Tigran occupying major Hellenistic centers, Hellenism was no longer on the fringes of Armenia, but penetrated most aspects of Armenian life. Tigran's marriage to Mithradates' daughter and the arrival of many Greeks in his empire, meant that Greek, together with Persian, became the language of the upper classes, while Armenian continued to be spoken by the masses. Greek theater became the main form of entertainment. Persian influence, however, remained in Tigran's court protocol and in the service required by nobles, neither of which had anything in common with either Greek or Roman traditions. When Sulla retired from public life in 79 B.C., new military commanders sought to advance their standing. The Roman Senate gladly authorized foreign campaigns in order to lessen civil unrest and to end the Mithradatic wars, a thorn in Rome's eastern ambitions. In 74 B.C. the Roman general Lucullus invaded Pontus and forced Mithradates to seek refuge in Armenia. Unwilling to break the Armeno-Pontic front against Rome, Tigran

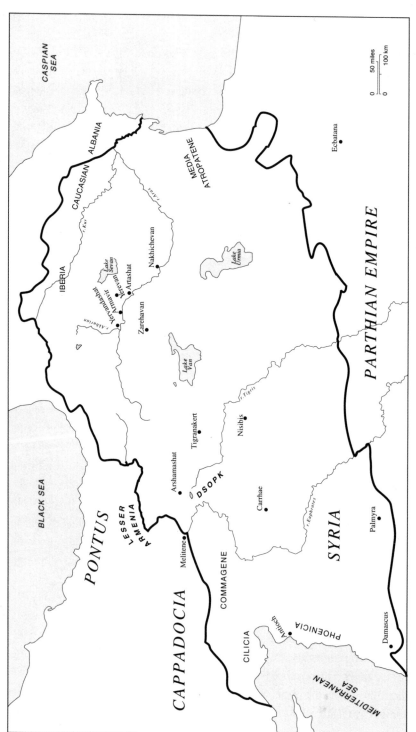

8. Armenian Empire (c. 80 B.C.)

refused to surrender his father-in-law and faced a Roman attack on Armenia. In 69 B.C. Tigranakert was besieged by Lucullus. When the city's inhabitants, a majority of whom were non-Armenians, opened the gates of Tigranakert, it fell to Roman troops and was looted. Tigran's local governors threw their lot with Rome, and Tigran lost control of Syria and Mesopotamia. Lucullus tried to take Artashat but failed, and, when he was unable to form an alliance with Parthia, returned to Rome. Tigran and Mithradates then began the reconquest of Pontus, northern Syria, and Commagene. Rome did not surrender its claim, however, and sent Pompey, who defeated Mithradates and forced him to flee eastward. Pompey then advanced toward Armenia. Having killed two of his sons for conspiracy against him, Tigran now faced the treachery of his third son, who first joined the Parthians and then defected to Pompey. The Roman presence in Armenia also incensed the Parthians, who wanted to ensure their control of the lands east of the Euphrates. In order to end the Armenian and Roman threats and to regain its territory, Parthia, taking advantage of Armenia's vulnerability, attacked from the east. Tigran resisted the Parthian attacks at Artashat, but when Pompey arrived, he realized the futility of resisting the Romans, and in 66 B.C. agreed to the Peace of Artashat. Pompey, in order to maintain Armenia as a strong buffer and a friend of Rome, while, at the same time, keeping Parthia in check, left Armenia intact and allowed Tigran to retain the Persian title, "King of Kings." Tigran ruled for another ten years and died in 55 B.C. Having resolved the situation in Armenia, Pompey pursued Mithradates, who committed suicide on an island in the Black Sea. Pompey then reorganized Asia Minor and Syria into Roman provinces and client kingdoms. Furthermore, he terminated the rule of the last Seleucid, probably a pretender, and closed a chapter in the history of the Hellenistic Middle East.

Armenians revere Tigran as their greatest ruler. He fashioned the only Armenian empire, a state which transformed Armenia from a small nation to a force with which to be reckoned. In their pride, the Armenians have mistakenly attributed nationalistic traits to Tigran. In fact, Tigran spoke Greek and Persian and had little of our modern sense of what it is to be Armenian. He was a Hellenistic monarch who, at the same time, retained much Persian grandeur at his court. He probably practiced polygamy, as was customary in Asia in this period. In all of this he was no different than any other contemporary ruler. Tigran's greatness lay in his attempt to forge an independent political identity and to break away from the constraints imposed on Armenia by geography. His early success was primarily due to the prevailing political vacuum and could not have been sustained. Tigran's empire was composed of various peoples who had been forcibly relocated and bore no love for the Armenians. Culturally, a fully-Hellenistic and urbanized Syria could probably not have co-existed with the more Persian-influenced and rural Armenia. Finally, Tigran's long reign fostered familial intrigue and the betrayal by his sons. Although Tigran's courage and efforts were indeed admirable, their outcome kept Armenia suspended between its stronger neighbors.

Artashesian Armenia after Tigran the Great

Tigran's remaining son, Artavazd II (55-35 B.C.), began his reign as a friend of Rome but under a very different political climate than had his father. With the demise of the Seleucids and Pompey's victories securing Rome's foothold in the Middle East, Rome's attitude became more that of conqueror than ally. Roman military presence in Syria and its aggressive interference in the affairs of Parthia led the latter to seek new friends in the region. Armenia, an immediate neighbor, located along Parthia's trading route and with ethnic, linguistic, and cultural ties, was drawn into the Parthian orbit.

The rivalry among Caesar, Crassus, and Pompey, who were known as the first triumvirate, precluded a consistent Roman policy in Asia. With the success of Julius Caesar's campaigns in Western Europe, the rich Crassus sought glory through a campaign against Parthia. Crassus' request for Armenian assistance placed Artavazd in a difficult situation. Any military cooperation with Rome would be viewed as a hostile act by the Parthians. Armenia, however, was considered an ally of Rome. Artavazd, according to some sources, advised Crassus not to attack Parthia from the direction of Syria, but rather through Armenia where he could receive supplies and support. Artavazd's strategy seemed to be to aid Rome, but demand in return a Roman military presence to protect Armenia against Parthian retaliation. Crassus, in haste, rejected

Artavazd's offer and marched through Syria. Artavazd then shifted his allegiance from Rome to Parthia, either voluntarily, or, according to Plutarch, by force, when the Parthians occupied Armenia. In 53 B.C. Crassus and the Roman legions were routed in the battle of Carrhae. Crassus was killed, and the Roman standards captured by the Parthians. The rapprochement between Armenia and Parthia was sealed by the betrothal of Artavazd's sister to the Parthian heir-apparent. According to Roman sources, Artavazd and the Parthian king were watching a Greek play at the wedding celebration when the head of Crassus was presented on a silver platter. Rome now distrusted Armenia, but Caesar's quarrel with Pompey and involvement with Cleopatra precluded any action to avenge Crassus and to recapture the Roman standards.

Artavazd, in the meantime, made every effort at friendly overtures to Rome, while remaining an ally of Parthia. Following the assassination of Caesar, a second triumvirate emerged in Rome, composed of Mark Antony, Octavian (later, Augustus), and Lepidus. In 41 B.C. Mark Antony, urged by Cleopatra, sought to strengthen his position in Rome by recapturing the Roman standards from Parthia. Like Crassus, Antony also demanded the assistance of Armenia. Artavazd initially cooperated with Antony, but in 36 B.C., when Antony's troops suffered a setback, Artavazd welcomed the Romans to winter in Armenia, but refused to commit troops for the war. Antony blamed Artavazd for his defeat and in 35 B.C. marched on Artashat and took Artavazd and some members of his family to Egypt, where Artavazd was later executed. Antony commemorated the "vanquishing of Armenia" by minting a coin for the occasion and, in a symbolic act, awarded Armenia to his young son by Cleopatra. Artashes II, a son of Artavazd, fled to Parthia and in 30 B.C., with Parthian help, took possession of his country by wiping out the entire Roman garrison. Artashes' death in 20 B.C. left Armenia open to different internal factions looking either to Augustus, now the emperor, or to Parthia. A number of Artashesians then ruled in Armenia, including a queen called Erato, whose image appears on a coin, as either Roman or Parthian clients. By around 10 A.D. the dynasty, after a period of power struggles, that eliminated many a contender, died out. The Roman empire under Augustus and his immediate successors then controlled Armenia for much of the first half of the first century A.D.

Society and Culture

During the Artashesian period, Hellenism made further inroads into Greater Armenia. Greek equivalents of Perso-Armenian divinities become more common. Zeus replaced *Aramazd,* Hephaestus replaced *Mihr,* Artemis replaced *Anahit,* Hercules replaced *Vahagn,* Aphrodite replaced *Astghik,* and *Tir* replaced Apollo. Artistic trends must have been similar to those found in Commagene, which blended Achaemenid and Greek traditions. Greek priests and cults undoubtedly brought numerous statues to Armenia, of which the bronze head of a goddess (some sources maintain that it represents *Anahit*) is the only surviving example. No painting or architectural monuments have been left from this period. The destruction of Hellenistic culture by both the Sasanids and the early Christians, and the numerous invasions of Armenia, have left few remnants. Despite Greek and Persian influences, Armenians continued to maintain their language and customs, a sign perhaps of nascent self-identity and fear of the assimilation which had befallen Commagene and Cappadocia.

Most of our information on this period is from numismatic and Roman sources. The latter were not necessarily objective on political matters involving the Armenians. The coins, especially those of Tigran the Great, depict the Armenian crown or tiara, which was unique in its design. The royal diadem was wrapped around a hat-like headgear in the form of a truncated cone decorated with birds on either side of an eight-pointed star; the crown had flaps which fell to the shoulders. The Armenian kings of this period, like most Hellenistic rulers, are depicted beardless. No literature of the period has survived but sources mention that famous Greeks sought refuge in Armenia and that Artavazd had written tragedies, orations, and histories. Greek plays were performed at Tigranakert and Artashat, and a number of Armenians studied in Rome, one of whom, called Tiran, became a friend of Cicero.

Trade formed the principal basis of the economy, especially during the reign of Tigran the Great. Plutarch mentions the great treasury at Tigranakert and the overall wealth of Armenia. There were mints in Tigranakert, Artashat, Damascus, and Antioch. Armenia maintained a standing army and did not employ mercenaries. The majority of the people were peasants, who were probably not fully bound to the soil as yet, but whose status was becoming increasingly serf-like. Land belonged to the king, the nobles, or the village commune. Slavery existed, but was not a significant institution and did not form the basis of the economy. The nobles or *nakharars* made their first appearance in this period. Tigran appointed some as governors of the outlying regions of his empire, while others, like the four great nobles or viceroys, served him at court. A somewhat fragmented administrative structure began to emerge at the end of the Artashesian period, which evolved into a feudal-like system and was to have a major impact on Armenian politics and society for the next fifteen centuries.

The first Armenian dynasty managed to survive for two hundred years and, for a short time, was a major power in the region. Roman involvement in Asia and the extension of its rule to the Euphrates, threatened the nearby capital of Parthia, Ctesiphon. The Parthians were unable to dislodge the Roman presence, and Rome would not relinquish its economic and political assets in the Middle East. The Artashesians first attempted to create a state powerful enough to challenge this dual threat. Its collapse led to an unsuccessful effort to balance relations with the two powers. At the dawn of the Christian era, the independence of the first Armenian kingdom became a casualty of the East-West rivalry in the region.

C.E.	ARMENIA	MIDDLE EAST & PERSIA	ROME & BYZANTIUM	INDIA, CHINA & JAPAN	SUB-SAHARAN AFRICA & THE AMERICAS
50	Corbulo invades Armenia (58-59) Peace of Rhandeia (64) Arshakuni dynasty (66-248) Trdat I (66-88) Vespasian establishes Roman authority in western Armenia (72)	Vologeses I (51-77) Kushans invade Parthia Jews revolt against Rome (66) Titus ends Jewish state (70) Rome persecutes Jews Jewish diaspora begins	Nero (54-68) Pliny the Younger (c. 62-113) Juvenal (c. 60-140) Trdat crowned in Rome (66) Death of Petronius (66) Tacitus (c. 55-115) Vespasian (69-79) Colosseum built (c. 80) Titus (79-81) Domitian (81-96)	Kushan Empire to 225 in northwestern India Yamato clan rules in Japan Paper invented in China (c. 50) Han dynasty continues its rule in China	Chauvin cult in Peru
100	Trajan invades Armenia (114-116) Vagharsh I (117-144) Vagharshapat built (c. 120-140) Roman-Parthian wars in Armenia (161-163) Vagharsh II (186-198) Khosrov I (198-216)	Roman-Parthian conflict in Mesopotamia (c. 115-211) Jews revolt (116, 132-135) Decline of Parthia Small-pox epidemics (c. 165)	Nerva (96-98) Trajan (98-117) Hadrian (117-138) Pantheon built (c. 120) Cults of Mithra, Cybele and Isis Galen (c. 130-200) Antonius (138-161) Marcus Aurelius (161-180) Small-pox epidemic Commodus (180-192) Severus (193-211)	Emperor Wu (140-186)	Mayan civilization (c. 100)
200	Trdat II (217-252) flees to Rome (252) Sasanid rule in eastern Armenia (c. 260-298) Narseh (272-293) Khosrov II (279-287) rules in western Armenia Khosrov II assassinated Trdat flees to Rome (c. 287) Peace of Nisibis (298) Trdat III (298-330)	Camels first used in Arabian desert (c. 200) Birth of Mani (c. 216) Sasanid dynasty in Persia (c. 224-651) Shapur I (240-270) Death of Mani (271) Narseh (293-302)	End of pax Romana (c. 200) Growth of serfdom (c. 200-500) Economic decline (c. 200-300) Barbarian invasions (c. 200-280) Roman jurisprudence completed (c. 200) Plotinus (Neo-Platonism) 204-270 Caracalla (211-217) Macrinus (217-218) Civil Wars (235-284) Philip the Arab (244-249) Diocletian (284-305)	Buddhism in China (c. 200-500) Fall of Han Dynasty (220) China ruled by various groups (220-589)	Bantu speakers expand through Central Africa (c. 200-900)

Table 5: 50 A.D. to 400 A.D.

C.E.	ARMENIA	MIDDLE EAST & PERSIA	ROME & BYZANTIUM	INDIA, CHINA & JAPAN	SUB-SAHARAN AFRICA & THE AMERICAS
300	Christianity official religion (c. 314) Khosrov III. Dvin founded (c.340) Arshak II (350-368) Parantsem (368-369) Pap (369-374) Arshak III (378-385) in western Armenia (385-390) Khosrov IV in eastern Armenia (385-389) Armenia partitioned (387) Vramshapuh (389-414) Western Armenia under Byzantine rule (c. 390-640)	Shapur II (309-379) Persia persecutes its Christians, Jews and Manicheans	Renewed persecution of Christians (303) Constantine (306-337) Edict of Milan (313) Constantinople founded (c. 315) Council of Nicea (325) Empire under joint rulers (337) St. Augustine (354-430) Julian (361-363) Jovian (363-364) Valens (364-379) rules in the east Theodosius (379-395) Christianity official religion of Roman Empire (380) Council of Constantinople (381) Roman Empire partitioned (395)	Classical period of Hindu civilization (c. 300-800) Gupta Empire (320-467) Indian culture spreads to Southeast Asia Japan invades South Korea (369) Kalidasa (c. 380-450)	Use of camels in African deserts (c. 300-500) Oaxaca Valley civilization in Mexico (c. 300-700) Kingdom of Axum in Ethiopia Spread of Christianity (c. 350) Moche culture in Peru

Table 5: 50 A.D. to 400 A.D.

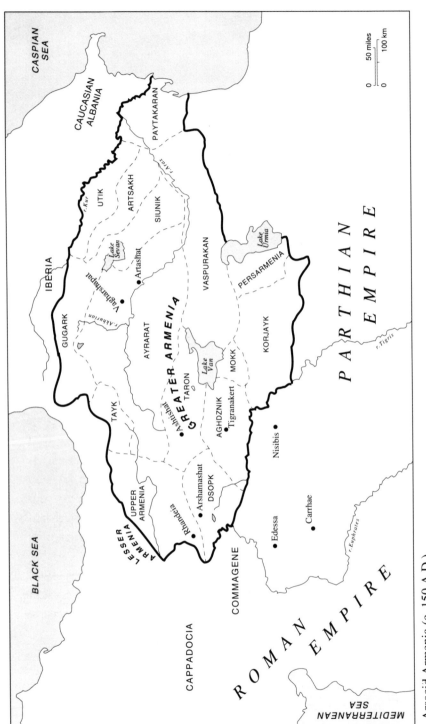

9. Arsacid Armenia (c. 150 A.D.)

VI

The Arsacid/Arshakuni Dynasty (66-428 A.D.) PART A

Parthian Body, Roman Crown: The Arsacids in Armenia (66-252 A.D.)

The final four centuries of the Classical Age was a glorious period for world civilizations. In the Americas, the Teotihuacan, Moche, and Mayan Civilizations were formed. In India, the Gupta dynasty ushered in the Indian classical age, spreading it to the far corners of southeast Asia. In China, the Han dynasty ruled for another two centuries. Its organized administration kept China culturally united, despite political fragmentation and nomadic invasions that lasted for over three centuries after their fall. The Yamato clan consolidated its rule over Japan, invaded Korea, and began selectively to adopt aspects of Chinese culture, including the ideographic script. The greatest changes, however, occurred in Persia and Rome. Although the Parthians managed to rule for another two centuries, they were plagued by nomadic invasions, quarrels among their nobility, epidemics, locusts, and attacks by Rome. In the early third century, they were replaced by a new and more powerful Persian dynasty, the Sasanid. The Sasanid state sought to purge Hellenism and replace it with pre-Alexandrian Persian religion and culture.

Rome, without doubt, left the greatest political and cultural mark on Europe and the Middle East. The empire, which had replaced the republic, was responsible for the *pax Romana*, a period of security, order, harmony, flourishing culture, and expanding economy. By the fourth century,

Christianity and the rise of the Eastern Roman empire assured the continuation of the Roman legacy for another millennium. The fate of smaller nations of the region clearly depended on Roman and Persian policy, as that of the Jews, who revolted against Rome and were forced into a two-thousand year diaspora. For the Armenians, the period culminated in the formation of their national religion and language.

Perso-Roman Rivalry in Armenia

Following the death of the Emperor Augustus in 16 A.D., the Arsacid rulers of Parthia, tried to weaken or altogether remove Roman control over Armenia and Mesopotamia. Lesser Armenia, which had gravitated into the Roman orbit during the reign of Augustus, fell firmly into Roman hands. The Romans then appointed a number of Armenian and non-Armenian rulers to govern it. The proximity of large Roman forces in the north and west threatened Parthia's security. Roman intrigues, as well as the demand for hostages by the Emperors Tiberius, Caligula, and Claudius, constantly disrupted the internal peace of Parthia. During the next fifty years, therefore, Armenia remained the scene of the conflict between Rome and Parthia. Roman, Iberian (Georgian), or other foreign governors ruled Armenia, while Parthia tried to install its own candidates, urging the Armenian population to rise against Rome. Armenian nobles living in the eastern part of Armenia soon gravitated to the Parthian sphere, while those living in the western part of Armenia continued to look to Roman governors in Syria for protection.

In 51 A.D., Vologeses I assumed the throne of Parthia and openly challenged Rome by seeking to obtain the throne of Armenia for his younger brother Trdat (Tiridates). The opportunity presented itself when the son of the Iberian king invaded Armenia and captured the fortress of Garni from his uncle, who was the Roman-appointed ruler. The Iberian aggression and looting, combined with Roman mismanagement, angered the Armenians and prompted Vologeses to invade Armenia and capture Artashat and Tigranakert. The arrival of winter, however, forced the Parthians to retreat, and the Iberian prince returned to wreak havoc on the Armenian population, who eventually rebelled against Roman rule altogether. The Parthians were then able to occupy Armenia and install Trdat as king.

The Emperor Nero, in 54 A.D., sent General Corbulo to take command of the army in Syria and to re-establish Roman control over Armenia. Corbulo raided Armenian regions which supported Parthia and encouraged the rulers of Iberia and Commagene to attack Armenia's borders. At the same time, the Parthians raided the Roman camps and threatened Roman supporters in Armenia. By 59 A.D., Vologeses had to contain internal revolts in Parthia, as well as deal with the growing strength of the Kushan state in the east, and left Trdat unsupported. The Romans invaded Armenia, burning cities and killing and enslaving the population. The capital city, Artashat, was burned to the ground by Corbulo, who also captured Tigranakert. Trdat fled to Persia, and Nero appointed Tigranes, a descendant of Herod the Great and the ruler of Lesser Armenia, as king of Armenia.

Corbulo left for Syria, and a new commander, Paetus, was appointed with orders to annex Armenia. The Parthians, having resolved their internal problems, moved to assert their claims. In 62 A.D., at Rhandeia, the Parthians surrounded the Romans, who agreed to withdraw from Armenia. Vologeses sent envoys to Nero proposing a compromise whereby Trdat would become king of Greater Armenia, but would receive his crown from Rome. Nero, who had hopes of another military victory by Corbulo, rejected the offer. Nothing came out of the Roman campaigns, however, and a stalemate ensued. Finally in 64 A.D., again at Rhandeia, Rome accepted the compromise of co-suzerainty. The Armenian kings would henceforth come from the royal Arsacid house of Parthia, while their authority would be bestowed by Rome. Trdat travelled to Rome and was crowned by Nero in great festivities as king of Armenia in 66 A.D. Nero gave funds to rebuild Artashat, which in his honor was renamed Neronia for a time. Greater Armenia and Dsopk were combined to form the Armenian Arsacid kingdom. Lesser Armenia remained a Roman vassal, ruled by a member of the house of Herod.

The Armenian Arsacids

In 66 A.D., Trdat I founded the Armenian branch of the Parthian Arsacids, which two centuries later would become an Armenian dynasty, known as the Arshakuni. The chronology of the Arsacid/Arshakuni dynasty is problematic. The Arshakuni kings left no coins — a key tool used by historians to date individual reigns — in all likelihood because the Armenians were not given the right to mint. Few sources on this period have survived due to the zealous eradication of Hellenistic culture by the Sasanids, who, as will be noted, had a particular hatred for the Parthian Arsacids and their Armenian kinsmen. Whatever monuments and sources did survive the Sasanids were destroyed by the early Christians.

The Armenian Arsacids began their reign by rebuilding Armenia. The fortress of Garni was repaired and a new temple added there by Trdat's sister. Parthian political, social, and cultural influences became dominant in Armenia. Aside from a threat from the Alans, a people who came down from the Caucasus, and a campaign against Iberia, nothing else is known of the reign of Trdat I. Trade between Asia and Europe revived and enabled Armenia to secure its independence. Although Parthia began its decline in the second century A.D., the Roman emperors who followed Nero (Galba to Nerva) honored his agreement concerning Armenia's kings. In 72 A.D., when the Alans overran Armenia and Parthia, the Emperor Vespasian decided to incorporate Lesser Armenia into the Roman province of Cappadocia and fortify its borders. It was the Emperor Trajan who broke the Rhandeia compromise and, in 114 A.D., when a civil war raged in Parthia, invaded Armenia. His justification was to restore the rightful king of Armenia who had been replaced by a candidate not approved by Rome. Although the unapproved candidate then presented himself and asked Trajan to crown him, Trajan refused, had him killed, and annexed Armenia as a Roman province. For the next three years Trajan remained in the east. By 116 A.D., the capital of Parthia, Ctesiphon, had also been captured, and Trajan crowned a new Parthian king, who became a Roman vassal. Rome thus extended its borders beyond the Euphrates and reached the Persian Gulf, the farthest extent of the empire, but the victory was short-lived. Military losses, rebellions, and the death of Trajan in Cilicia in 117 A.D. forced the new Emperor Hadrian to move back to the former Euphrates border; the Rhandeia compromise was restored when another Parthian prince, Vagharsh I (117-140 A.D.), assumed the throne of Armenia. During his long reign trade and prosperity were restored and the city of Vagharshapat, or present-day Edjmiadsin, was founded.

Social Structure of Arsacid Armenia

The social structure of Armenia, in the meantime, had changed. Trdat and the subsequent Arsacid rulers of Armenia had brought Parthian nobles and family members into Armenia where they had settled on newly-created fiefs. Other noble families continued to immigrate to Armenia, especially after the fall of the Arsacids of Persia. Among these families were the Mamikonians and the Kamsarakans. Greek language, gods, theater, and other aspects of Hellenism were familiar to the upper classes of both Armenia and Parthia. The Parthians nobility thus felt at home and inter-marriages among the aristocracy became common. Persian and Parthian were also spoken, and the Aramaic script gradually gave way to the Parthian script, a derivative of Aramaic. More Persian words found their way into the Armenian vocabulary. Most of the two thousand Persian loan words and derivatives in classical Armenian are from this period and relate mainly to war, hunting, trade, court, and political structure.

Rome, as noted, could and occasionally did challenge the Parthian choice for the Armenian throne by invading or even annexing Armenia. The only way to assure continuity of government and discourage Roman interference was to adopt the Parthian custom of appointing the high-ranking nobles to hereditary court and administrative positions and assigning them fiefs in exchange for military service, thus creating a loyal nobility, whose position and lands would depend on the Arsacids. Armenia was eventually divided into fifteen provinces. There emerged an elaborate hierarchy headed by the king, who was first among equals, and who ruled the central province of Armenia. Below him were the nobles, known as *nakharars*. The *nakharars'* rights to their lands and titles were inalienable and were inherited through the law of primogeniture. The major *nakharars* could muster up to ten thousand cavalry troops in time of war. The standing army of the Artashesians had thus been replaced by a feudal force. Four of the *nakharars* were given the title *bdeshkh* (viceroy or margrave), and were granted vast domains and responsibility for guarding the northern and southern borders of Armenia. The remaining ten provinces of Greater Armenia were under the control of other *nakharars* (see map 9). To keep tight control over the *nakharars*, the king, as was later customary in Western feudalism, appointed them to court offices. The office of coronant, for example, was given to the Bagratuni family; the Mamikonians became the *sparapet*, or commanders of the armed forces; the Gnunis became the *hazarapet*, or officials in charge of taxation and food production. There was also a *mardpet*, or royal chamberlain, who was in charge of the king's palace, treasury, and household. The *mardpet* was always a eunuch, implying the existence of a royal harem.

The *nakharars* were not all equal, and their rank was indicated by their place or cushion at the royal table, another Parthian custom. The list of ranks, called *gahnamak*, obviously varied from time to time. After the *nakharars* came the *sebuhs*, or minor princes, and the *azats*, or the knights, who held small fiefs from the king or *nakharars* and who formed the cavalry. These four groups were all exempt from corporal punishment, and with the exception of the *azats*, from taxes. The rest of the society fell into the category of *ramik*, which included city dwellers and enserfed peasants (*shinakans*). The *ramik* served as the infantry in time of war and paid the bulk of the taxes. The artisans and traders, some of whom were foreigners, lived in the cities. The institution of slavery was, by this time, waning.

The second century of Arsacid rule in Armenia saw the continuation of the Roman-Parthian rivalry and periodic threats from the Iberians and Alans. The *nakharars*, aided by the mountainous terrain, kept their regions well-defended and, together with Parthian assistance, kept Armenia autonomous. After Vagharsh, a number of Roman and Persian candidates ruled Armenia. In 186 A.D., another Parthian prince named Vagharsh became king of Armenia (Vagharsh II). In 191 A.D. he left Armenia to assume the throne of Persia and named his son Khosrov as king of Armenia (Khosrov I). Khosrov, who ruled during the time of the Roman Emperors Septimus Severus and Caracalla, had to face renewed Roman expansion in Mesopotamia. Khosrov was captured by Caracalla, who sent Roman officials to govern Armenia. Neither Rome nor Parthia, however, expected what followed: the Armenians rose up in arms and defeated the Roman general sent to quell them. The Armenian population was by the early third century, apparently tired of Roman interference in their affairs. More importantly, the Arsacid rulers who had remained in Armenia for a period of time had become Armenian and considered Armenia their homeland and, the Armenians, likewise, viewing Parthian customs and language as closer to their own, and their rule more lenient, favored them over the Romans. By a new agreement between Rome and Parthia, Khosrov's son, Trdat II (217-252 A.D.) was crowned king of Armenia. Following the established tradition, he received his crown from the Roman Emperor, in this case, Macrinus. Trdat II, however, was the first Arsacid king who was raised in Armenia and who followed his father as king of Armenia. His long reign, combined with the civil wars in Rome, would have enabled Armenia to take a respite from East-West rivalry and to found a separate Armenian dynasty at the start of the third century; however, around the year 224 A.D., an event occurred which transformed the Middle East and severed Armeno-Persian political and religious ties.

PART B

The Cross and the Quill: The Arshakunis (279-428 A.D.)

The Sasanids and Armenia

Arsacid power in Parthia began to wane in the second century. Roman policy in Syria was to encourage its military governors to continually interfere in Persian politics in order to undermine the Arsacids, a strategy which largely succeeded. A virulent smallpox epidemic added to the general economic drain of warfare, and so weakened the power of the Arsacids that, in 224 A.D. they were overthrown by Ardeshir, the founder of the Sasanid dynasty.

The Sasanids differed in several fundamental respects from their predecessors in Persia, a fact which had significant consequences for

Armenia. The Sasanids kept their administration highly centralized and held to the memory of Armenia as part of the Persian kingdom of the Achaemenids. A stronger adversary against Rome than Arsacid Persia had been, Sasanid Persia did not hesitate to violate the agreement of Rhandeia and to act unilaterally regarding Armenia. The Sasanids' fervent promotion of Persian Zoroastrianism as the official religion of the empire meant not only the persecution of other religious sects in Armenia, but the eradication of Hellenistic culture in Persia, and to some extent, in Armenia. No longer able to rely on its Arsacid kinsmen in Persia, Armenia had to depend solely on Rome for protection. Sasanid rule did benefit the Armenians in one respect: Armenia could now install members of its own royal family as kings, creating a truly Armenian Arshakuni dynasty. That the Arshakunis managed to rule under the Sasanids for two centuries is due to their own political skills, intermittent Roman aid, and two events, which united the Armenian people unlike anything before, the establishment of Christianity and the development of the Armenian alphabet.

Trdat II had to rule in the face of this new factor in the Roman-Persian struggle for control of Armenia and Mesopotamia. Armenia cooperated with Rome during the campaigns of Emperor Severus Alexander to forestall Ardeshir's expansion. By 244 A.D., however, the situation had changed drastically. The great Sasanid king Shapur I (240-270 A.D.) defeated the Roman emperor Gordian in Mesopotamia. He then made peace with Emperor Philip, who agreed not only to pay a ransom and an annual tribute, but also to renounce Roman protection of Greater Armenia. Sixteen years later, Rome was to be humiliated further by the defeat and capture of Emperor Valerian by Shapur in Carrhae, Syria. In 252 A.D. Shapur invaded and occupied Armenia. Trdat II probably fled to Rome at this time, and Shapur incorporated Armenia into the Persian empire, placing his own son, Hurmazd, on the throne of Armenia. Hurmazd ruled Armenia until his father's death in 270 A.D. when he left to assume the Persian throne and was replaced by his brother, Narseh, who ruled Armenia until 293 A.D. Persia's strength and direct Sasanid control over Greater Armenia, while interrupting the independent rule of the Arshakunis, did have the benefit of bringing an extended period of peace to Armenia.

Roman fortunes improved after the death of Shapur, and by the end of the third century, Rome, under Diocletian, managed to reassert its influence in the western parts of Greater Armenia and Mesopotamia. A compromise with Persia allowed Rome to revive the Armenian Arshakuni dynasty and to install King Khosrov II, who seems to have ruled in the western provinces of Greater Armenia between 279 and 287 A.D. The Sasanids, however, who continued to view all of Armenia as their domain, plotted against Khosrov and the pro-Roman *nakharars* through the king's brother, who murdered Khosrov, and who, with other pro-Persian Armenians, cooperated with the Sasanids to reassert control over all of Greater Armenia. Khosrov's son, Trdat III, either escaped to Rome or was already in Rome, where, as other sons of Rome's allies, he was being educated in Roman customs. Khosrov's murderer became the ruler of Greater Armenia when, in 293 A.D., Narseh left to govern Persia. Trdat, meanwhile, remained at the court of Diocletian until Rome defeated Narseh in 298 A.D., and Trdat, backed by a Roman army, reclaimed his murdered father's throne. By the Peace of Nisibis (Mdsbin), Persia and Rome once again agreed to an independent Arshakuni Armenia as a buffer state. The Armenian borders, however, were once again rearranged. Most of Dsopk was separated from Greater Armenia. Its *nakharars* became independent *satraps* and allies of Rome. Lesser Armenia was expanded southward, detached from Cappadocia, and made into a separate province. Diocletian's abdication, division within the empire, and Constantine's efforts to unify it, kept the Romans occupied during the early years of the fourth century. Armenia was left unprotected at a very crucial period, for the Sasanids had gained another strong king in Shapur II (309-379 A.D.). Shapur renewed Persian attacks on Armenia and Syria and encouraged Zoroastrian proselytizing in Armenia, bringing the local cults in line with orthodox Zoroastrianism by destroying statues and prohibiting idolatry. It is against this backdrop, during the reign of Trdat III, known as Trdat the Great, that Armenia became the first state to adopt Christianity as its official religion.

Christianity in Armenia

One of the most crucial events in Armenian history was the conversion of Armenia to Christianity. By adopting the new religion in the fourth century, Armenia renounced its Eastern or Persian-influenced past, established a distinct Christian character of its own, and, at times, became identified with the Western world.

The traditional account of the conversion is based on a mixture of facts and fiction recorded a century later by the Armenian chronicler known as Agathangelos. It tells of the wars of an Armenian king Khosrov (probably Khosrov II) against the new Persian Sasanid dynasty and the efforts of Persia to destroy the Armenian Arshakunis. The Persian king employed a traitor named Anak (in fact, probably Khosrov's brother) to murder the Armenian king. Promised a reward by the Sasanids, Anak settled in Armenia, befriended Khosrov and murdered him and most of his family. Anak and his family were, in turn, slain by angry Armenian courtiers. Only two sons were saved from death: Khosrov's son Trdat (probably Trdat III), who was taken to Rome, and Anak's son (the future Gregory the Illuminator), who was taken to live among Christians in Cappadocia.

Years later, according to Agathangelos, Trdat, with the help of Rome, returned to Armenia to regain his father's throne. Passing through Caesarea he met the son of Anak, who had been given the name of Gregory by his Christian mentors, and, unaware of his true identity, took him into his service. After regaining Armenia, Trdat, recognizing great abilities in Gregory, raised him in stature at court. Gregory, of course, had already accepted the Christian faith and eschewed pagan ceremonies. Soon rumors of his parentage began to surface, spread by jealous nobles, which lead to his torture and imprisonment in Khorvirap ("deep pit"). Years passed and Trdat, like his godfather Diocletian, continued his persecution of Christians. Among the martyrs of that period were Gayané and Hripsimé, two virgins who had refused Trdat's advances and were put to death. According to Agathangelos, Trdat was punished for his sins by turning into a wild boar. No one could cure him of this transformation until his sister, Khosrovidukht, had a dream in which an angel instructed her to release Gregory, who, despite long years in isolation, had, by divine intervention, survived in the pit. Gregory healed the king, who, in 301 A.D., proclaimed Christianity the sole state religion, making Armenia the first Christian state. Gregory then travelled to Caesarea to be ordained by the Greek bishop there, an action which would later have serious repercussions for the Armenian Church. Upon his return Gregory baptized the king and all the Armenian nobility, destroyed pagan temples, and in their place erected churches and shrines to the Armenian martyrs. At Vagharshapat, on a spot shown to him by Christ in a vision, he built the great cathedral of Etchmidzin ("the spot where the Only Begotten Son descended").

This legendary tale was accepted until modern times as accurately describing the forces motivating Armenia to become the first state to adopt Christianity. Like most tales, however, it does not explain the entire story nor give a correct chronology of events. To understand the reasons for the Christianization of Armenia one should look at political and social developments in Persia, Rome, and Armenia during the previous century. Although available historical data is scarce, scattered, and confusing, it is clear that it was external pressures which gave the Armenian throne the impetus to unite its people behind Christianity.

Christianity, as an underground and forbidden religion, was practiced in the Roman provinces of Palestine and Syria, particularly in the city of Edessa, from where it had spread to southern Armenia as early as the first century. Another Armenian tradition claimed that a certain king, Abkar of Edessa, had asked Jesus to come to his kingdom to cure him of an illness. After the resurrection, the Apostles Thaddeus and Bartholomew went to Edessa to spread Christianity in Syria. Thaddeus then went to Armenia where he preached and was martyred by order of the Armenian king. It is out of this tradition that the Armenian Church claims an Apostolic heritage. By the second century, Armenia had a number of underground Christian cells in the southern and western provinces which had secured the protection of some local nobles. By the third century Christianity was practiced in Armenia, albeit still in a semi-secret manner, along with Hellenistic and pre-Hellenistic beliefs, and another dualistic belief, Manicheanism. According to Eusebius, there was an Armenian bishop called Mushegh, who in 250 A.D., had corresponded with Christians in Alexandria. It is probable that Gregory, who was originally from a Parthian family, came in contact with Christians in Armenia during the second half of the third century.

The situation changed drastically after the Sasanids transformed

Zoroastrianism from a religion of the upper classes into the official religion of Persia. An official orthodoxy emerged, fueled by zealous missionary activity, which threatened Armenia's political, as well as religious, identity. In the Roman empire, on the other hand, overt Christian persecutions had eased with the departure of Diocletian, and Christianity had increased in popularity in Syria and the eastern provinces of the Roman empire. In 313 A.D., Emperor Constantine issued the Edict of Milan, in which he excused Christians from pagan rituals and granted their religion the same tolerance accorded to all others. In Christianity, to which already a substantial number of Armenians had converted, Armenian leaders found a religion both tolerated by their strongest ally and possessing a messianic fervor strong enough to counter Zoroastrianism. Thus, soon after, probably in 314 or 315 A.D., and not in 301, the traditionally-held date, Armenia was politically ready to become the first nation to officially adopt Christianity as its state religion. More than half a century later, in 380 A.D., Emperor Theodosius finally declared Christianity the state religion of the Roman empire.

Although paganism persisted for some time and even resulted in the martyrdom of a number of Armenian Church leaders, the new Christian religion was forced upon everyone. Hellenistic temples were destroyed and churches were built over them, much as early Roman churches were later built over pagan shrines. Following Gregory's vision, the great temple of *Anahit* in Vagharshapat as noted was replaced by the cathedral of Etchmidzin. Christian missionaries spread the new faith throughout Armenia, Georgia and Caucasian Albania. These efforts assured the permanency of Christianity as the religion of Armenia and a deterrent to Persian dualistic religions.

Church organization followed the feudal system. The position of the catholicos, or the supreme patriarch of the Church, was inherited for a time by the family of Gregory the Illuminator. Bishops were chosen from among the *nakharar* families. The lower clergy was included in the *azat* class and received fiefs from bishops in return for service. The bishops and priests served as judges, with the catholicos as the supreme judge. The Church became a major power in Armenia and helped to create a distinct Armenian identity. Almost a century later, the creation of the Armenian alphabet would further strengthen that sense of identity.

Armenia and the Councils of Nicea and Constantinople

In 325 A.D., during the reign of Trdat III, the emperor Constantine summoned the First Ecumenical Council of the Christian Church to meet at Nicea in Asia Minor. Gregory's son, Aristakes, represented Armenia. The council's main objective was to define the Christian creed and to resolve the controversy between Arius and Bishop Alexander of Alexandria. Arius maintained that Christ was not of the same substance as God, hence not divine, while Alexander, and his successor Athanasius, maintained the doctrine of one substance. While the council rejected Arianism there were some bishops who were unwilling to accept all the decisions of Nicea. Keeping the bishops divided would assure the continuing power of the emperor over the Church, and so, Constantine and a number of his successors allowed the Arian debate to continue. Armenian kings followed the example of the Byzantine rulers and clashed repeatedly with the leaders of their own Church. It was not until 381 A.D., when the Emperor Theodosius accepted the rulings of the Second Ecumenical Council at Constantinople which confirmed the Athanasian creed, that the Armenian and the Greek Churches finally reconciled with their monarchs.

Arshak II

The fourth century was a tumultuous period for Armenia. The seventy year-long reign of Shapur II and his attempts to dislodge the Roman presence from Armenia and Mesopotamia ravaged the Armenian economy. The political and socioeconomic condition in Armenia enabled the *nakharars* to play a major role in domestic policy. Some *nakharars* favored Rome, others Persia, while others pursued their own independent course.

As with much of the chronology of the Arshakunis, there is no clear data on the rulers between Trdat III and Arshak II. Khosrov III (known as "Kotak" or "Short") is mentioned in a number of sources as ruling from 330 to 338 A.D. and constructing a new capital at Dvin. More is known about the reign of Arshak II. Some historians argue that Arshak II began his reign in 338 A.D., although it is more probable that he commenced his rule in 350 A.D., after Shapur's third campaign against Rome. Nearly all that is known about Arshak is from Church sources, which, as will be seen, had reasons for painting an unflattering portrait of the ruler. Arshak seems to have been put on the throne as a compromise between the Emperor Constantius II and Shapur. The royal court rarely resided in the new capital city of Dvin during Arshak's reign; rebuilding and reorganization became the first item on his agenda.

Reconstruction and regulation were on the Church's mind as well. The new catholicos, Nerses I, of the Gregorid house, called the first Armenian Church council at Ashtishat. As a result, hospitals and orphanages were established, and the practice of pagan and Zoroastrian rituals forbidden. During this period, married men were permitted to join the ranks of the upper clergy, providing that they no longer lived with their wives. In time, however, there developed a two-tiered hierarchy of celibate upper clergy and non-celibate lower clergy.

Arshak, following the example of the Byzantine emperors, maintained a pro-Arian position, and when Nerses objected, Arshak replaced him with a more cooperative catholicos. He then tried to bring the feudal lords under his control by having those who opposed him killed. Arshak retreated with his followers to the new city of Arshakavan, which was soon, however, destroyed in a rebellion. Arshak's problems were compounded by his marriage to the widow Parantsem, whom he married, according to some accounts, while his first wife was still alive; others accuse him of murdering his first wife in order to marry her.

Arshak's position was bound to the Roman presence in western Armenia, and as long as Rome managed to resist Shapur, he was secure. When Shapur II defeated the Emperor Julian, however, and forced the Emperor Jovian to yield western Armenia in 364 A.D., Arshak's fate was sealed. The king and his general Vasak Mamikonian were ordered to Persia where they were blinded, tortured and killed. Parantsem resisted heroically, but, she too, lost her life, while Arshak's son Pap escaped to Pontus. Shapur sacked a number of Armenian cities, took thousands of prisoners to Persia, and once more made Armenia into a Persian province. Zoroastrian temples were erected, replacing some churches. Two pro-Persian nakharars, who were related to the Persian royal house and who had probably converted to Zoroastrianism, were assigned to govern Armenia as Sasanid vassals.

The Partitioning of Armenia

Rome could not tolerate a Persian-dominated Armenia and, in 367 A.D., the Emperor Valens, who had become the ruler of the eastern provinces of the Roman empire, supplied funds and troops to Pap and the Armenian general, Mushegh Mamikonian. The Armeno-Roman force defeated the Persians at Bagavan. Pap asked Catholicos Nerses to return and tried to reconcile with the Church and the *nakharars*, but like Valens and his own father before him, Pap was pro-Arian. Conflict with the Church and the *nakharars* ensued; Nerses was soon murdered and the majority of *nakharars*, including Mushegh Mamikonian, turned against the king. The *nakharars* in Dsopk, who had maintained their independence since the Nisibis agreement, abandoned the king and declared the five districts of Dsopk, renamed as the Pentarchy or the southern satrapies, as an independent region under the protection of Rome. In 374 A.D., Pap was murdered with the acquiescence of Rome. Pap's successor, his nephew, did not rule long and was replaced by the Mamikonian house, whose rule was short-lived. Fortunately for Armenia, Shapur died in 379 A.D., while the Roman empire was soon divided into Western and Eastern (Byzantine) branches (see map 10). The Mamikonians eventually restored the Arshakuni throne to the two young sons of Pap, but retained close ties to the center of power, by marrying them to Mamikonian women.

Arshak III, the younger son of Pap, was forced by pro-Persian *nakharars* to flee in 385 A.D. to the western part of the country, and to seek Byzantine protection. The *nakharars* then elevated a pro-Persian Arshakuni prince, Khosrov IV, as the king of Armenia. Tired of a long war which had resulted in a stalemate, Emperor Theodosius and Shapur III, in 387 A.D., decided to partition Armenia. Byzantium received the smaller portion, stretching west of Theodosiopolis (present-day Erzerum) in the north and Martyropolis in the south and including the much-Hellenized Lesser Armenia. Arshak III, remained on as king and a vassal of Byzantium. Persia received most of Greater Armenia, including the cities

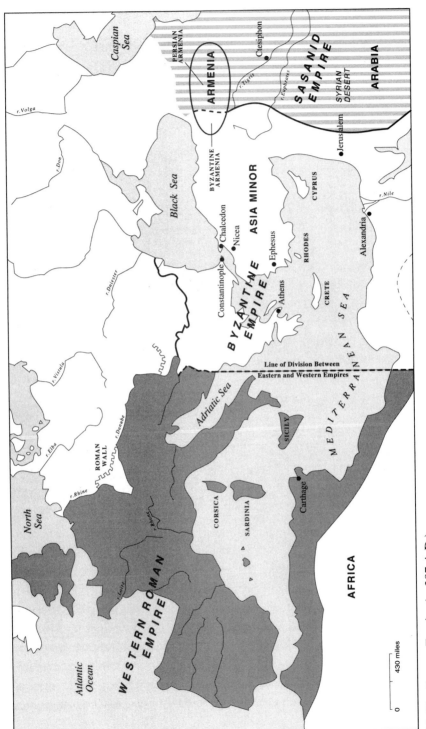

10. The Roman Empire (c. 387 A.D.)

of Artashat and Dvin, and Khosrov IV continued as king and a vassal of the Sasanids. To further weaken Armenian political and economic power, the Persians stripped Greater Armenia of six of its provinces: Gugark was made part of eastern Georgia, Artsakh and Utik were made part of Caucasian Albania, and Paytakaran, Korjayk, and Persarmenia joined Persia proper (see map 11).

Upon the death of Arshak III, the Byzantines did not appoint another Armenian king and the Arshakuni line in Byzantine Armenia came to an end. Some of Arshak's *nakharars* left for Persian Armenia, the rest became Byzantine vassals. Greek governors and culture began to make inroads in Byzantine Armenia. In Persian Armenia, Khosrov IV was succeeded by Vramshapuh (389-417 A.D.), who nominated Sahak, the last catholicos of the Gregorid line. Vramshapuh is a significant figure in Armenian history, as a motivating force behind the creation of the Armenian alphabet.

The Development of the Armenian Alphabet

The most momentous event of the Arshakuni period was the invention of the Armenian alphabet. Prior to the fifth century, Armenians used Greek for artistic and cultural expression, Latin and both versions of Middle Persian (Pahlavi) scripts for official communications and inscriptions, and Syriac for their liturgy. Because the majority of Armenians could not read or write, Armenia had a rich oral tradition. History was not recorded, but recited from memory and sung by Armenian and Persian *gusans* or minstrel-poets.

Both the crown and religious leaders of Armenia saw the partition of Armenia as an event of devastating potential. Both realized the perils to an Armenia under Byzantine and Persian administrative and religious control. The fledgling Armenian Church faced other problems as well. On the one hand, the influence of the Syrian Church, whose own liturgy was used by the Armenians, was increasingly encroaching upon the authority of the Armenian Church. The ecumenical councils, on the other hand, foreshadowed the future ecclesiastical domination of Byzantium in the region. Moreover, contrary to popular tradition, Christianity did

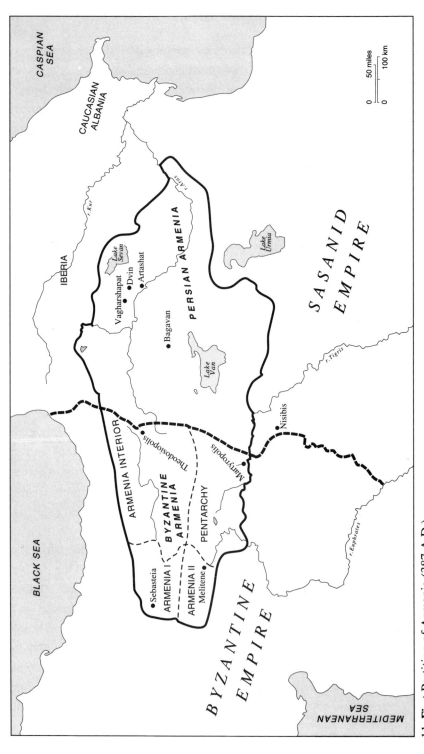

11. **First** Partition of Armenia (387 A.D.)

not take hold of the entire population at once; paganism and Zoroastrianism still commanded many followers and converts.

Both Catholicos Sahak and Vramshapuh realized that in order to retain any measure of ecclesiastical and political control over a partitioned nation, the unifying factor of the Armenian language would be crucial. They asked Mesrop Mashtots, a learned scholar and clergyman, to create an alphabet which would distinguish Armenia, linguistically and liturgically, from the powers surrounding it. Mashtots, who was born in the province of Taron, had studied Greek and Syriac, and was employed by the *hazarapet* in the royal secretariat. According to his student, Koriun, who wrote a biography of his master in the mid-fifth century, Mashtots had been well-versed in secular law and military arts before devoting himself to the religious life. He had travelled all over Armenia and fully recognized the threat of assimilation. Mesrop and a number of his students travelled, examined different alphabets, including earlier attempts at an Armenian alphabet, and consulted calligraphers. Using Greek, Syriac, and letters from other scripts, Mashtots, sometime between the years 400 and 405 A.D., shaped the thirty-six letters of the Armenian alphabet. To give the new alphabet a divine aura and make it more acceptable, legends were circulated which claimed that the alphabet was bestowed on Mesrop in a divine vision. The miracle, however, was the alphabet itself, which represents the many distinct consonant sounds of Armenian and which has remained virtually unchanged for 1500 years. Mesrop's students opened schools throughout the Armenian provinces to teach the new alphabet. Fortunately, the Sasanid monarchs during these years happened to be extremely tolerant, as was Emperor Theodosius II, who permitted Mesrop's students to run schools in Byzantine Armenia as well. Armenian tradition maintains that Mesrop then went on to develop alphabets for the Georgians and the Caucasian Albanians as well.

Immediately thereafter, Armenians entered upon a period of translating major Christian and philosophical texts into Armenian. The first work to be translated was, not surprisingly, the Bible. The translation was made from the Syriac and Greek versions and is highly regarded by Biblical scholars. The catholicos and king enthusiastically supported the efforts of priests and scribes to translate and copy the writings of the early Christian fathers, the canons of Church councils and various liturgical works. Armenians who had studied at Athens, Edessa, Nisibis, and Antioch, and who were familiar with the works of Greek grammar, logic, philosophy, and rhetoric, translated Porphyry, Diodochus, Probus, and other Neo-Platonic philosophers, among others. Aristotle was a particular favorite as shown by the more than three hundred manuscripts of his works in archives in Yerevan.

The translators left a legacy for Western civilization as well, as a number of Syriac and Greek texts have been preserved only in their Armenian translations. Hippolutus' *Commentaries on the Benediction of Moses*, the complete text of Ephraim's *Commentary on the Diatessaron*, the first part of the *Chronicle* of Eusebius, Timothy Aelurus' (Patriarch of Alexandria) *Refutation of the Definition of the Council of Chalcedon*, and *The Romance of Alexander the Great* by Pseudo-Callisthenes are among them. During the high Middle Ages and the Renaissance, when Western Europe was "rediscovering" the literature and culture of the classical world, these Armenian translations formed an important link to the knowledge of the past.

The Armenian translators began their large output in the fifth century and continued until the second half of the seventh century, when the Arab invasions somewhat slowed their pace. Original works, including histories, were written after the fall of the Arshakunis in 428 A.D. and will be discussed in chapter VII.

Trade, Art and Architecture

The only pre-Christian monument surviving from this period is the complex at Garni. The temple, built in the first century A.D., was destroyed by an earthquake in 1679 and was restored over a decade ago. Parts of the original fortifications, the Garni fortress and a bath have also been preserved. Garni also provides the only example of the decorative art of the period in the form of a mosaic in the bath depicting sea gods and fish. A number of crude reliefs and carved heads from tufa, representing unknown Arshakuni kings, are all that is left of the sculptural art of this period. The first churches in Armenia were constructed at Vagharshapat, Ashtishat, and near Lake Sevan. These were single-nave edifices, often built upon the foundations of pagan temples which had been destroyed by the early Armenian Christians. Some of the temples were simply converted outright by relocating the apse to the traditional east side. In the fifth century, as will be noted, a number of central-domed cathedrals and domed basilicas began to appear. Few of the early churches constructed in the fourth century have survived. The mother cathedral of Armenia, Etchmidzin, although dating from this period, was totally rebuilt in the late fifth century and expanded throughout its history. The church of Ereruk, which is also of this period, like other early Armenian churches located on the territory of the Armenian Republic, is being restored; however, those in Turkey, Nakhichevan, Azerbaijan, Persia or Georgia, have, with some exceptions, been left in ruins.

During the Arsacid and Arshakuni periods, trade flourished along the route from Ctesiphon to Armenia and the Black Sea, enabling merchants and artisans to sell their wares in Rome and Persia. The route went from Ctesiphon to Armenia and the Black Sea, and the cities of Artashat, Dvin, Nakhichevan, and Theodosiopolis became major trade centers between India, Iberia, Persia, and Europe. Dvin in particular became a entrepôt where merchants met to transact business.

After the death of Vramshapuh, the Sasanids installed first, a Persian prince to rule Persian Armenia and later, a son of Vramshapuh, Artashes IV, who ruled until 428 A.D. The *nakharars*, preferring to rule themselves, successfully requested that the king be deposed and that Catholicos Sahak be replaced. Armenia thus became a land divided between Byzantium and Persia, with no national leader. Prior to the Sasanids, the Armenian kings, who were related to the Persians, had to deal primarily with Rome. After the Sasanids took over Persia, Armenia once again had to maneuver between the mighty Roman and Persian empires, resulting in its partition and the termination of its second dynasty. The incessant and violent struggle between Persia and Byzantium and the appearance of the Arabs would subject Armenia to fragmentation and leave it leaderless for over four centuries. But the Armenians had gained three powerful weapons: a new religion, a script, and regional leaders, all of which would enable Armenia to weather the coming storms.

C.E.	ARMENIA	MIDDLE EAST & PERSIA	ROME & BYZANTIUM	INDIA, CHINA & JAPAN	SUB-SAHARAN AFRICA & THE AMERICAS
400	Alphabet invented (c. 400) Artashes IV (422-428) End of Arshakuni Dynasty (428) Marzpan period (428-638) Vardanank Wars (c. 440-484) Battle of Avarayr (451) Nuvarsak agreement (484) Armenians reject Chalcedon (491 and 506)	Tolerance for certain Christians in Persia Bahram V (420-438) Yazdgird II (438-457) Peroz (459-484) Talmud completed (c. 480) Balash (484-488) Mazdakism in Persia (c. 490)	Pope Innocent I (401-417) Barbarian invasions (c. 410-470) Council of Ephesus (431) Pope Leo I (440-461) Attila in Europe (c. 450) Council of Chalcedon (451) Fall of Western Roman Empire (476) Boethius (c.480-524) Merovingian rule begins (481) Clovis adopts Roman Christianity (496)	Japan adopts Chinese ideographs (c. 400) Fa-hsien in India (405) White Huns in north India (c. 480-600)	Classical Mayan civilization in Central America (c. 500) Settlements in Ghana (c. 500) Apex of Teotihuacan civilization in Mexico
500	Justinian's edicts in Armenia (535-536) Armenian calendar commences (552) Council of Dvin (554) Partition of Armenia (591)	Khosrow I (531-579) Brief revival of Sasanids Birth of Muhammad the Prophet (c. 570) Khosrow II (591-628)	Decline of towns and trade in the West (c. 500-700) Benedictine order founded (c. 520) Justinian (527-565) Maurice (582-602) Pope Gregory I (590-604)	Glass, compass, gunpowder in China (c. 500) Buddhism in Japan (552)	

Table 6: 400 A.D. to 600 A.D.

VII

Fire Temples and Icons:

Armenia Under Persian and Byzantine Rule (428-640 A.D.)

The more than two centuries between the collapse of the second Armenian kingdom and the arrival of the Arabs coincided with the eclipse of the ancient world and the dawn of the early medieval period. The Western Roman empire fell and fragmented, gradually to emerge as various kingdoms throughout Western Europe. The kingdom of Soba rose in Africa. The great Indian Gupta empire fell to invaders from the north. Buddhism reached Japan, and China finally restored its imperial order under the Sui and T'ang dynasties. The Eastern Roman empire, or Byzantium, continued its struggle against Sasanid Persia in Armenia and Mesopotamia. The intolerance of both the Zoroastrian and Greek hierarchy affected the other religious groups who lived in the Middle East. Furthermore, continual warfare left both Persian and Byzantine resources depleted. Such conditions prepared the ground for the rise of a new political and religious force, that of the Arabs and Islam.

The spread of Christianity, the invention of the Armenian alphabet, and the growing autonomy of the *nakharars* appeared at an extremely crucial period. Armenia, now partitioned, would need all the national identity it could muster to survive the more powerful cultures which controlled its destiny. This was especially true by the mid-fifth century, when the short reigns of the more tolerant Sasanid and Byzantine rulers came to an end. The Persians and the Byzantines employed different strategies in administering their respective Armenian provinces. During the more than two centuries following the partition, therefore, the two Armenias faced very different political, religious, and socioeconomic conditions.

Persian Armenia

Persian Armenia, with its capital at Dvin, was ruled by a governor of the frontier or *marzpan* (*marzban*) appointed by the Sasanids. The *marzpan* commanded the local garrison and had full authority in administrative, judicial, and even religious matters. He was assisted by a *hazarapet*, who had more authority than the earlier *hazarapets* of the Arshakuni period. A *magpet*, or chief of the magians (Zoroastrian priests), resided at Dvin. Tax officials lived in every district of Armenia and a special supervisor oversaw the Armenian gold mines. Besides being the administrative and religious capital, Dvin also became a center of trade, with both the Persians and Byzantines viewing Armenia as a passage for their caravans. Weaving, pottery, and jewelry made in Armenia were exported to neighboring regions.

Armenian *nakharars* still controlled many highland areas and for the most part remained autonomous, paying taxes to the Persians and receiving their appointment from the Persian king. A number of prominent *nakharars* were granted the position of *marzpan*, and the *sparapet*, a Mamikonian, continued to lead the *nakharar* military contingents. Sources describe the magnificent palaces and jewels and garments worn by the Armenian *marzpan* and other high officials which duplicated those of Persian counterparts. Many Christians lived in the Persian empire, especially in Mesopotamia and western Persia. Once Byzantium accepted Christianity as its own, however, Christians, even heretic sects, living under Persian rule, were viewed as a threat and were occasionally persecuted. The Armenian Church leadership was also appointed by the Persian throne. The Gregorid house, suspected by both the Persians and *nakharars* of espousing the restoration of the kingdom and a more centralized Armenian government, was removed, and other candidates, including several non-Armenians, were given the title of catholicos. As a result of Persia's control over ecclesiastical affairs, the Church lost contact with the West and became increasingly isolated from its fellow

Christian Churches. This isolation was to have historical consequences in the years that followed.

Council of Ephesus

In 431 A.D., another heresy, Nestorianism, prompted the Christian Church hierarchy to call a Third Ecumenical Council, this time at Ephesus. Nestorius, the Patriarch of Constantinople, believed in the separate character of Christ's human and divine natures. Although the council condemned Nestorianism, the debate continued and two decades later resulted in the first division of the Christian world. The Armenian religious hierarchy at Etchmidzin was still under Persian control at this time and was probably not represented at the Council of Ephesus. Following Ephesus, Nestorians were welcomed in Persia as enemies of Byzantium. The Sasanids, at times, viewed the Armenian Church as part of the Nestorian Church in Persia.

The Vardanank Wars

For the first fifty years following the partition, Armenia was generally left alone in its religious and cultural affairs and held its own Church councils. The situation altered drastically in 439 A.D. with the ascension of Yazdgird II to the throne. He and members of his court attempted to impose Zoroastrianism on all of the non-Persian peoples living in his empire. When Armenia resisted, taxes were increased and some *nakharars* were sent to fight Central Asian nomads threatening Persia. The final blow came when the Persian king dispatched Zoroastrian priests to convert the population. Armenian peasants and especially residents of Dvin were angered at the arrival of Zoroastrian priests sent to build a fire temple in the capital. Some of the *nakharars* and churchmen gathered at Artashat in 447 A.D. and declared to the king that, although they were faithful to Persia, they were also faithful to their Church. The reaction of another group of *nakharars*, however, was not as strong. A pro-Persian faction sought a dialogue and compromise with their overlords. These were led by the Armenian *marzpan*, Vasak Siuni, whose family had occasionally held the position of viceroy, and who viewed himself as a prince of the Armenian people. His mountainous domain bordered Persia, and his two sons were hostages at Ctesiphon. In opposition to him were most churchmen, a large part of the population, and many other *nakharars*, all led by *sparapet* Vardan Mamikonian.

Resistance to the Persians continued on a minor scale for a decade. By 450 A.D. the Armenians were in open rebellion against the Persians and, together with the Georgians and Caucasian Albanians, who were under similar pressures from Persia, defeated a Sasanid army. In search of a stronger ally, the Armenians sought aid from Constantinople. The aid from Byzantium did not materialize, while Vasak and his followers continued to oppose the rebellion, which they no doubt viewed as detrimental to their official status as representatives of the Persians. In 451 A.D. the main Persian army met the rebels on the plain of Avarayr in Artaz (present day Maku, Iran). Vardan Mamikonian and his entire army perished, becoming martyrs of the Armenian Church. Vasak Siuni did not join the battle and has been accused of treachery ever since by Church historians. In his own day, however, he, along with the pro-Persian *nakharars*, was held responsible for the insurgency and imprisoned by the Persians.

The death of Vardan and his stand against more powerful forces elevated him, and the rest of the fallen heroes, to the status of Christian and national martyrs and gave them an importance which they did not possess in life. Accounts of the battle circulated and helped rally the population against the Persians. Persian persecutions, the arrest of neutral and even loyal *nakharars*, and the execution of a number of priests stiffened Armenian resolve and local Armenian resistance. The Sasanids must have been surprised at the persistence of the Armenians, for Yazdgird soon released many of the *nakharars* and pursued a more lenient policy in Armenia. During the next two decades, however, the Armenians sought vengeance for the martyrs of Avarayr with a series of rebellions in Armenia and Georgia. Supported by the Armenian Church, the conflict became known as the Vardanank Wars. In 481 A.D., the rebels under the leadership of Vahan Mamikonian, took Dvin, the seat of the *marzpanate*, and defeated a Persian army in 482 A.D. Disagreements with Georgia led to Armenian losses and forced Vahan Mamikonian to continue his struggle as a guerilla for a year. In the meantime the Sasanids had their own internal problems. They were attacked by nomadic invaders, faced disputes over the succession, and had to deal with the heresy of Mazdak and his followers, who espoused communistic and ascetic doctrines. As a result, in 484 A.D, peaceful relations were restored when Vahan Mamikonian was named *sparapet* and regained his fief in exchange for the support of a Sasanid candidate to the throne. Armenia was granted freedom of religion and the right to appeal to the Persian court directly, bypassing the *marzpan*. A year later Vahan himself was named *marzpan* and ruled for two decades. Interestingly, the agreement, known in Armenian sources as the Nuvarsak treaty, is not mentioned in Persian sources, indicating that either the Armenian rebellion was considered a minor incident in Persian history or that none of the Persian sources on it have survived. Nevertheless, Armenians today celebrate Avarayr and Nuvarsak as moral victories. They view the struggle as a symbol of the survival of their identity against powerful forces. After the death of Vahan, the next eight Armenian *marzpans* who ruled intermittently continued to face pressures from the Zoroastrians until the Arab invasions.

Following Nuvarsak a period of reconstruction began. Both the *nakharars* and the Church managed to reorganize and rebuild Armenia. Vagharshapat and Dvin were restored. Armenia revived economically as trade once again began to pass to Byzantium. Despite some disruptions during the Perso-Byzantine wars and the invasions of the Huns, Armenia's revival continued until the mid-sixth century.

The Council of Chalcedon

In the meantime, the Fourth Ecumenical Council met at Chalcedon in 451 A.D. The council decreed that Christ's two natures were not separate as Nestorius claimed, or confused as Eutyches maintained, but united without confusion, change, or division. A number of Eastern Churches, the Coptic and Ethiopian among others, led by the patriarch of Alexandria, rejected Chalcedon's Dyophysite decrees as a version of Nestorianism, and hence a heresy. They maintained that Christ had only one, divine nature and became known as Monophysite Churches. Christian religious leaders, realizing the seriousness of the situation, tried to find a way to reconcile the dissenting groups. In 482 A.D. they convinced

Emperor Zeno to issue the Act of Union or the *Henoticon*. The Act recognized the religious foundations of the first three ecumenical councils as entirely sufficient. It stated that "Christ was of the same nature with the Father in the Godhead and also of the same nature with us in the manhood." The terms "one nature" or "two natures" were avoided. Although at first the compromise appeased the leaders of the Monophysitic Churches, it was soon rejected by both the Monophysites and Dyophysites. The Monophysites viewed it as too vague and the Dyophysites saw it as a concession to Monophysitic doctrine. The Armenians, because of the Vardanank struggle and the battle of Avarayr, which took place in the same year as Chalcedon, did not attend the council. The canons of the council and Zeno's *Henoticon* only gradually arrived in Armenia, in various versions. It was only in the late fifth century, after the Persian threat had subsided, that the Armenian bishops, in 491 A.D., gathered in Vagharshapat and rejected the decision of Chalcedon. A few years later (506 A.D.), in Dvin, they, along with the Georgians and Caucasian Albanians, reiterated their objections. Zeno's *Henoticon* was not rejected, however, and helped to maintain a dialogue between the Armenian and Greek Churches. The decision was a prudent one, as a third of Armenia was still under Byzantine administration. The Armenian Church, at the same time, insisted that it was not Monophysitic, but rather followed its own unique interpretation which viewed the two natures of Christ as indivisible. Although the humanity of Christ was not emphasized, it was not altogether ignored. Many religious experts classify the Armenian Church as Monophysite. Viewed through strict Monophysite doctrine, however, the Armenians are not true Monophysites; taking a more lenient definition, Armenians come close to holding a Monophysitic doctrine. Was the decision to reject the Council of Chalcedon political or religious? Probably both. It is likely that the Armenian bishops, realizing that western Armenia was already coming under Byzantine control, feared that their Church would eventually be engulfed by the powerful hierarchy at Constantinople. The apostolic tradition of the Armenian Church, after all, had long been challenged by the Greeks, who claimed that since Gregory had been ordained by the Greek bishop of Caesarea, the Armenian Church was subordinate to the Patriarch of Constantinople. The Persians, at the same time, were extending tolerance to Nestorians and other heretical Christian groups. By affirming both a unique doctrinal position and their apostolic tradition, the Armenians maintained their national Church and identity. Pressures from Byzantium continued for the next few decades and increased during the reign of the Emperor Justinian. Armenians were finally forced to break with Constantinople. In 552 A.D. the Armenian Church adopted its own calendar and in 554 A.D., at the second council of Dvin, the Armenian Church considered a complete break from Constantinople, a decision which by 609 A.D. became official and resulted in the establishment of a national Armenian Church.

Byzantine Armenia

The Byzantines gradually tried to transform Byzantine Armenia into a territory resembling the rest of its empire. Lesser Armenia, already under the firm control of the Byzantium military commander, the *Dux Armeniae,* and partially assimilated, was subdivided into the administrative units of Armenia I, with its capital at Sebasteia (Sivas) and Armenia II with its capital at Melitene (Malatya). The western part of Greater Armenia, which had been awarded to Byzantium in the partition of 387 A.D., became known as Armenia Interior, where a civilian governor known as the *Comes Armeniae* held a position equivalent to the Persian *marzpan* (see map 11). The Byzantine governor there relied on the few *nakharars* left in the region to gain the cooperation of the population. A number of *nakharars* and princes such as the Mamikonian and Arshakuni families held their own domains but paid taxes and supplied troops to Byzantium. Until Chalcedon, the Christian Church was unified and Greek remained the literary language of the upper classes. The *nakharars* were left to themselves and, for the most part, served the imperial administration. The *nakharars* in the southern districts of Armenia Interior, the region of Dsopk, now known as the Pentarchy or the southern satrapies, in particular, were viewed as allies and a buffer against Persia, and, as noted, were independent from Byzantine military or administrative control. Persian pressures on their Armenian population also gave the Byzantines a more positive image. These conditions contributed to the gradual assimilation of Lesser

Armenia and parts of Byzantine Armenia. There were no challenges to rally the people, no overt threats to their national identity. The introduction of the alphabet and the subsequent literary and educational activity, however, combined with the independent stand of the Armenian Church, changed the atmosphere. The situation worsened when *nakharars* in the Pentarchy, who had close ties to Constantinople, rebelled in 485 A.D. It is possible that either the Armenian rebellion and resistance in Persian Armenia motivated these *nakharars* to rebel as well, or that they were enticed by promises from Persia. Following the rebellion, Byzantium annexed the Pentarchy and placed it under the same status as the rest of Armenia, to be governed by imperial officials.

Although under separate rule, Persian and Byzantine Armenia had numerous channels of communication. Trade from China and Persia passed through Artashat and Nisibis into Byzantine Armenia. Persian Nestorians maintained a large theological school and translation center at Edessa in Byzantine territory, and Armenians from the Persian zones studied there as well. Intermarriage between Armenians living on the borders of the two areas was common, and travel, although restricted, was permitted. The Emperor Zeno began the first major changes in Byzantine Armenia. He introduced a number of Roman laws into Armenia Interior, to bring it into line with Armenia I and II, and ordered stricter control of the border. The school at Edessa was closed, forcing its relocation to Nisibis in the Persian empire. Byzantine spies increased their activities in the border regions, forcing the Persians to restrict movement. The Byzantines especially wished to break the Persian monopoly over Chinese silk, a material in great demand at the imperial court. Byzantium's hostile actions and refusal to pay their share of expenses to guard the passes in the Caucasus against nomadic incursions, started new armed conflicts with Persia. The wars (503-505 A.D. and 524-531 A.D.) were fought in Byzantine Armenia and Mesopotamia, and although they went against Byzantium, internal problems in Persia hampered them from taking full advantage of Byzantium's weakness. In 531 A.D., however, Sasanid Persia resolved its Mazdakite problem by killing Mazdak and his followers, and its succession disputes, when Khosrow I executed all of his own brothers and their male offspring, save one. In 533 A.D. Khosrow, known as Anushirvan, finally concluded an "endless peace" with the Emperor Justinian, in which the Byzantines had to pay large sums of gold toward the upkeep of the Caucasian defenses and keep a low offensive profile on its eastern borders.

Byzantine Armenia in the Period of Justinian

Having resolved his war with Persia, Justinian began his reorganization of the empire, initiating major changes in Byzantine Armenia. In 536 A.D., he decreed that all the various administrative offices in Armenia were to be abolished and combined under a single military command (*Magister militum per Armeniam*), headquartered at Theodosiopolis. New fortifications separating Byzantium and Persia created a Byzantine Armenia virtually sealed-off from its neighbor. Residents of the two Armenias could no longer intermingle or maintain any degree of unity through commercial or cultural interaction. Justinian divided Byzantine Armenia into four administrative units: First Armenia (Inner Armenia plus most of the former First Armenia) with its capital at Theodosiopolis; Second Armenia (the rest of the former First Armenia plus additional territory in the northwest) with its capital at Sebasteia; Third Armenia (the former Second Armenia) with its center at Melitene; and Fourth Armenia (the Pentarchy or southern satrapies) with Martyropolis as its center (see map 12). Governors and tax collectors resided in each region to assure the incorporation of Byzantine Armenia into the rest of the empire. The *nakharars* lost their autonomy, and the Byzantines introduced legal measures to assimilate the Armenians as much as possible. Roman law was fully extended to all of Byzantine Armenia, with serious consequences for the *nakharars*. Under Roman law daughters and younger sons could inherit. Thus the Armenian *nakharars* who had kept their lands intact for generations under the leadership of the eldest male member of the house, or *tanuter*, were now forced to divide them among their children. The *nakharar* lands would eventually be split into powerless small holdings. A number of Armenian nobles rebelled, Byzantine officials were murdered, and some *nakharars* even turned to Persia for help. These *nakharars* were either deported to the Balkans or were drafted into the Byzantine bureaucracy. Armenian assimilation, which had began earlier, continued during the sixth century. Byzantium's

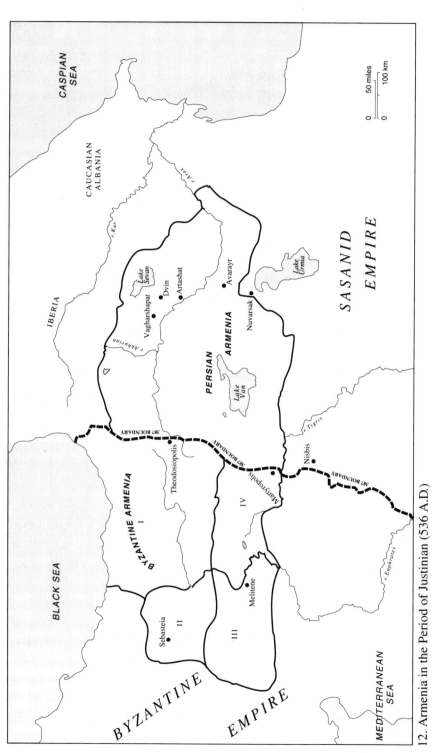

12. Armenia in the Period of Justinian (536 A.D.)

armed fortresses on the border, its expansionist policy, and especially its smuggling in the secret of silk production, angered Khosrow. Requests from Armenian *nakharars* in the Byzantine zone encouraged the Persians to start a new war in 540 A.D., which dragged on until 562 A.D., when a fifty-year truce was established by which Persia would bear the cost of guarding the Caucasian passes but would receive an annual tribute in gold from Byzantium.

Perso-Byzantine Conflicts and the Second Partition of Armenia

The situation for both Armenias had worsened by the last quarter of the sixth century. In 571 A.D. the Persian *marzpan* built a fire-temple in Dvin. The Persian Armenians rebelled under the leadership of another Vardan Mamikonian, known as "Red" Vardan and sought the protection of Justin II. The emperor, who did not wish to pay the large annual tribute in gold to Persia, broke the truce in 572 A.D. He offered to aid the Persian Armenians, but when the war turned against Byzantium, Justin abdicated and his successor, in 575 A.D., came to terms with Khosrow in order to retain parts of Mesopotamia. Vardan and a number of Armenian *nakharars* and their retinue fled to Byzantium. This truce did not last either, however, and the two antagonists again fought in Byzantine Armenia. The Emperor Maurice (582-602 A.D.) was more successful in fighting the Persians. He ordered a scorched earth policy on the borders with Persia, creating a vast no-man's land at the expense of both Armenias. The Armenians who had lost their homes in those regions were then deported to Cyprus. Maurice saw a chance to extend Byzantium's borders when Khosrow II, known as Parviz, was deposed in 591 A.D. by Bahram Chubin. In the same year, Maurice intervened and helped the Persian prince to regain his throne. Byzantium's newly-acquired prominence in the internal affairs of Persia now enabled it not only to annul the annual tribute, but to receive a large part of Persian Armenia. The boundary between the two sectors now ran from the northeast corner of Lake Van up the Hrazdan River to the northwest corner of Lake Sevan. Dvin remained in the Persian zone but Yerevan fell to the Byzantine side. The additional territories were named Inner, Lower and Deep Armenia. To complicate matters, the Byzantines renamed their former Armenian holdings. First Armenia became Greater Armenia, Second Armenia remained the same, Third Armenia was renamed First Armenia and the term Third Armenia fell out of use; and Fourth Armenia was referred to as Ioustiniana, and encompassed the Pentarchy as well as additional territory in the north and east (see map 13). Both Maurice and Khosrow carried out a policy of depopulating Armenia and sending the *nakharars* to various parts of the empire or to fight in Africa, Central Asia, or the Balkans.

The murder of Maurice and his sons by Phocas in 602 A.D. started a new war with Persia. Khosrow II soundly defeated the Byzantines and came within a mile of Constantinople. The war continued after the death of Phocas and the ascendancy of Heraclius in 610 A.D. By 620 A.D., the Persians had conquered all of Armenia, the Middle East, most of Asia Minor, and claimed to have captured the True Cross from Jerusalem. The situation in Byzantium was desperate when the Emperor Heraclius decided to use his navy to transport troops closer to the Persian lines. The Byzantine offensive of 622 A.D. proved successful and by 628 A.D. Asia Minor, the Middle East, and Armenia were in Byzantine hands. Khosrow II was killed by his own troops and his son made peace with Hercalius, returned the True Cross, and restored the 591 A.D. agreement and borders. From then on, the Sasanids were in no position to threaten Byzantium and rapidly declined.

Heraclius realized the strategic importance of Armenia far better than any of his predecessors. In order to concentrate on the now frequent Avar and Slavic raids on the western borders of Byzantium, he required a strong ally and a secure Armenia on his eastern flank. Therefore, he created the position of "prince of Armenia" and chose not a Mamikonian, but a member of a minor *nakharar* family to control the administration of Armenia. The man he chose was Theodore Rshtuni, who was to play a significant role in the next period of Armenian history.

Literature, Learning and Art

The two centuries of devastation, deportation and the disruption of trade affected both Armenias, particularly Byzantine Armenia. It is surprising

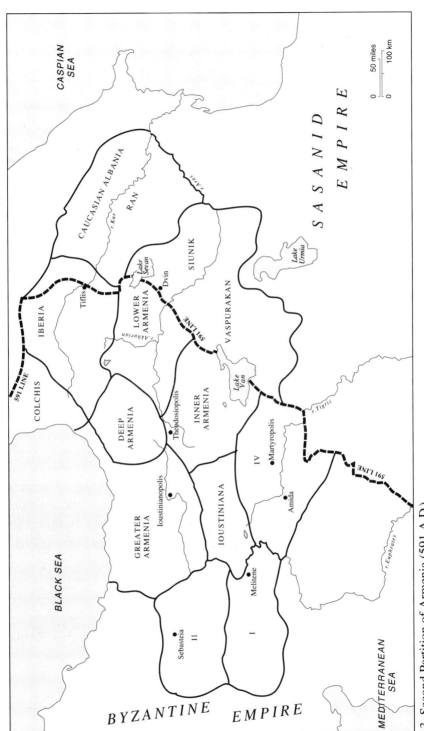

CASPIAN SEA

SASANID EMPIRE

50 miles
0
100 km
0

CAUCASIAN ALBANIA

RAN

r. Araxes

Lake Sevan

SIUNIK

Lake Urmia

IBERIA

Tiflis

LOWER ARMENIA

Dvin

VASPURAKAN

591 LINE

r. Akhurian

COLCHIS

591 LINE

DEEP ARMENIA

Theodosiopolis

INNER ARMENIA

Lake Van

r. Tigris

IV

Martyropolis

591 LINE

Ioustinianopolis

IOUSTINIANA

Amida

GREATER ARMENIA

r. Euphrates

BLACK SEA

IOUSTINIANA

Melitene

II

I

Sebasteia

BYZANTINE EMPIRE

MEDITERRANEAN SEA

13. Second Partition of Armenia (591 A.D.)

that artistic, scientific and literary activities not only continued throughout these centuries, but blossomed.

Architecture found its expression in the numerous churches constructed in this period. Basilican and cruciform central-domed structures
were used throughout this period. The Cathedrals of St. John in Mastara,
Avan, St. Hripsimé, and the Churches of Odzun, St. Gayané, and Aruj
are all from this period. A number of architectural historians originally
maintained that the Armenians were the first to translate into stone the
dome on corner supports. This notion has been replaced by new opinions
which maintain that similar structures were designed in different countries
at the same time. Nevertheless, the fact remains that Armenian architectural designs influenced Georgian, Caucasian Albanian, and Balkan
church architecture. In sculpture there are a few reliefs, a good example
being in the church of Ptghni detailing the founder of the church, an
Amatuni *nakharar*, hunting a lion. There are only a few examples of
painting, the most important of which is an illustrated gospel which subtly
blends Byzantine and Sasanid art into a unique Armenian style.

Political and socioeconomic conditions in Persian Armenia were more
favorable for literary activity, but the Byzantine side also contributed
with the many Greek philosophical and scientific works which were
translated into Armenian.

In the field of science, seventh-century Armenia produced Anania
Shirakatsi (Ananias of Shirak) who studied mathematics with a Greek
teacher at Trebizond and, upon returning to Armenia, wrote books on
arithmetic, chronology, weights and measures, the lunar cycle, geography, and cosmology. His information on the geography of Transcaucasia
and Persia, the trade routes, and the weights and measures used in Persia
have provided rare and valuable information for historians.

Literature, particularly original Armenian works in history, theology
and philosophy, made this period a very important one; indeed most of
the fifth century is referred to as the "Golden Age" of Armenian literature.
The earliest historical work was probably that of Pavstos Buzand (Faustus
Buzand), whose *History* describes the events of the fourth century up to
the partition of Armenia in 387 A.D. The author was a great supporter
of the Mamikonians and provides valuable information on Persia and
Byzantium. His work was either written in the fourth century in Greek

and translated into Armenian in the next century, or, written in Armenian during the fifth century. David Anhaght wrote original philosophical treaties, as well as commentaries on Greek philosophical works. Eznik of Koghb wrote his treatise *Against the Sects* in which he refuted Zoroastrianism, Manicheanism, and Gnosticism. The historian Agatangeghos (Agathangelos) wrote the *History of the Conversion of Armenia*; Koriun composed the biography of his teacher, Mesrop Mashtots. The Battle of Avarayr and events from the period of 430 to 465 A.D. are chronicled in Eghishe's moving *History of Vardan*. The division of Armenia and the Armenian struggle against Zoroastrianism during the years 384-485 A.D. are described in the *History* of Lazarus of Parpi (Ghazar Parpetsi). The most ambitious work of this period is that of Moses of Khoren, whose *History* begins with the origins of the Armenian people and ends in 440 A.D. There has been a lively scholarly debate on Khorenatsi's work, some scholars maintaining that this work could not possibly have been written in the fifth century and was composed at least three centuries later, and others arguing that it is indeed from this period. In any event, despite its many chronological inaccuracies, the work is a wealth of information on the early period of Armenian history.

The immense literary and translation activities of this period served as the key ingredient in the rise of national consciousness and in the Armenian struggle against both Persian and Byzantine cultural and religious pressures. Moreover, it prepared the Armenians for an even more important challenge, the Arab invasions and the arrival of Islam.

C.E.	ARMENIA	ISLAMIC MIDDLE EAST	BYZANTIUM & THE WEST	INDIA, CHINA & JAPAN	SUB-SAHARAN AFRICA & THE AMERICAS
600	Break with Orthodox Church (609) Heraclius in Armenia (623-627) Arab invasions and conquest (640-650) Rshtuni-Mu'awiyah agreement (652)	Hijra—start of Muslim calendar (622) Death of Muhammad (632) Age of the Caliphs (632-661) Muslims conquer Egypt (641) End of the Sasanid empire (651) Sunni-Shi'i split (656) Umayyad Dynasty (661-750) Mu'awiyah (661-680) Battle of Karbala (680) Martyrdom of imam Husein	Heraclius (610-641) Decline of the Merovingian Kingdom	Sanskrit drama (c. 600-1000) Stone temple architecture in India (c. 600-1200) T'ang Dynasty in China (618-907) Hsuan-Tsang in India (629) Taika reform Edict starts Imperial rule in Japan (645)	Tiahuanaco-Huari period in Peru Rise of cities (c. 600) Egyptian and Ethiopian Coptic Churches gain power (c. 650) Slave trade from sub-Saharan Africa to Mediterranean Sea (c. 650-1400)
700	Arabs create the province of Arminya (700-702) Massacre at Nakhichevan (703) Paulician movement in Armenia Church council at Dvin (719) Church council at Manzikert (725) Armenians rebel against Arab rule (774-775) Rise of the Bagratunis Ashot the Meat-Eater (790-826)	Height of Islamic commerce and industry (c. 700-1300) 'Abbasid Dynasty (750-1258) Harun al-Rashid (786-809)	Agrarian economy in the West (c. 700-1300) Muslims conquer Spain (711) Muslim siege of Constantinople (717) Iconoclasm in Byzantium (726-843) Muslims defeated at Tours (732/733) Boewulf (c. 750) Irish "Book of Kells" (c. 750) Frankish kingdom revived (751) Charlemagne (768-814) Song of Roland	Muslims reach Indus river (712) Nara period—first capital in Japan (710-784) Korea unified Golden age of Chinese poetry Heian period in Japan (794-1185)	Height of Mayan Civilization in Copan, Central America (c. 700) Soba and Dongola states Decline of ancient civilizations in the Americas
800	Tondrakian movement in Armenia (c. 840-850) Armenians rebel against Arab taxes (850-851) Bugha in Armenia (851-853) Samarran captivity (853-861) Ashot Bagratuni Prince of Princes (862-884) Ashot I, King of Armenia (884-890) Smbat I (890-914)	al-Khwarazmi (800-847) al-Amin (809-813) al-Ma'mun (813-833) Babak's revolt (816) Turkish mercenaries in Baghdad al-Mu'tasim (833-842) Capital moved from Baghdad to Samarra (836-870) Rise of Afshin (836) al-Mutawakkil (847-861) al-Mu'tamid (870-892) al-Razi (865-925) al-Kindi (d.870) Rise of Sufism Sajids in Azerbaijan	Carolingian Renaissance (800-850) Height of Byzantine trade and industry (c. 800-1000) Breakup of Carolingian Empire (850-911) Basil I (867-886) Alfred the Great in England (871-899) Height of Viking raids in the West (880-911)	Rise of Japanese culture Flowering of literature Khmer empire in Kampuchea (802)	

Table 7: 600 A.D. to 900 A.D.

VIII

A People of the Book:

Armenia Under Arab Domination (640-884 A.D.)

The two and a half centuries of Arab occupation of Armenia coincided with the Muslim conquest of the entire Middle East, North Africa, Spain, Sicily, and Cyprus. Europe, after its initial shock at the extent of Muslim success, finally managed to slow their progress by defeating the Arabs at Constantinople and Tours. Towards the end of this period, Europe attempted to resurrect the Roman empire when Charlemagne was crowned as emperor. India saw the height of Sanskrit drama and the period of its finest stone architecture. It resisted initial Muslim attacks from Sind and established the short-lived Harasha kingdom. The T'ang dynasty of China firmly established itself as the new power there. Japan, following the Taika Reform Edict, created its imperial government. In the Americas, the Mayan civilization was at its height, and the Tiahuanaco-Huari era began in Peru.

The Arab Invasions of Armenia

The Arab invasions, which began with raids in 640 A.D. and culminated in the domination of most of Armenia in the late eighth century, altered for the first time the ethnic composition of Greater Armenia. None of the previous invaders or conquerors had settled in Armenia. Rather, the earlier aggressors had come to loot or to establish political control over the Anatolian or Mesopotamian region which separated their empires from those of their rivals to the east or to the west. They represented organized and centralized bureaucracies and empires, whose citizens were not willing to abandon their own homes and culture and settle in a foreign land. The Arabs were different, however. Their forces were recruited from among many tribes. A number of these received fiefs from the central government and settled in Syria, Mesopotamia, Persia, and Armenia. For the next eight centuries, other nomads such as the Kurds, Turks, Mongols, and Turkmen would follow the Arab example. As they began settling in Armenia, the Armenians, in turn, emigrated, a situation which significantly affected the subsequent history of Armenia.

Unlike the speedy conquest of Persia, it took the Arabs half a century to subjugate Armenia. Armenia's mountains and its decentralized and partitioned hierarchy and administration assured pockets of long-standing resistance. The early raids began in 640 A.D. and succeeded in capturing Dvin. Theodore Rshtuni, who had been appointed by Emperor Heraclius as prince and governor of Armenia, and who, a year earlier had united Persian and Byzantine Armenias into a single entity, resisted further Arab raids for two years. In 644 A.D., a larger Arab army beat back an Armeno-Byzantine force. The Byzantines blamed Rshtuni for the defeat and attempted to replace him. At the same time, the Byzantine emperor, taking advantage of the Arab campaigns in Persia and Armenia, tried to impose the decisions of Chalcedon on the Armenian Church. Rshtuni and Catholicos Nerses III, known as the Builder, called a Church council at Dvin and, in 649 A.D., rejected these efforts.

The Umayyads and Armenia

In 650 A.D., the governor of Syria, Mu'awiyah, sent a large army which penetrated most of Armenia. Rshtuni defended Vaspurakan and hoped for either Sasanid or Byzantine action against the Arabs. What Rshtuni faced, however, was continued Byzantine demands for acceptance of the canons of Chalcedon as a pre-condition for any assistance and the collapse of the Sasanid empire before the Arabs. In 652 A.D. Rshtuni, together with a number of *nakharars*, made the fateful decision to make peace with the Arabs.

The agreement with Mu'awiyah was not unfavorable for the Armenians. Armenia was exempted from taxes for a number of years. In time of war Arabs could rely on the Armenian cavalry, which the Arabs agreed to maintain. No Arab governors would be posted to Armenia, and if Byzantium attacked, Arab troops would protect Armenia. Armenians would pay the *jizya* or poll tax, but as "a People of the Book" they were also guaranteed freedom of religion. Rshtuni thus managed to obtain something from the Muslims which he had been unable to wrest from the Christian emperor of Byzantium.

The rise of this new force in the Middle East meant significant political changes for Armenia, not all of them to her detriment. With the Sasanid empire destroyed and the Byzantine empire pushed back west of the Euphrates, there would be, for the first time in one thousand years, no significant East-West struggle in or over Armenia. Moreover, for the first time since 387 A.D., Greater Armenia was united under one rule and its people considered a single group by their overlords. Unfortunately it also meant that the Armenian noble families such as the Bagratuni, Mamikonian, Gnuni, Kamsarakan, Artsruni, Amatuni, Siuni, and Rshtuni would struggle among themselves to gain the title of prince of the Armenians.

The treaty between Damascus and Rshtuni angered the Byzantines and their Armenian supporters. The Mamikonians and the catholicos rejected the pact and joined a Byzantine force in ousting the Rshtunis, who sought refuge in the mountains of Siunik. Mu'awiyah dispatched a new army, which then forced the Byzantines to retreat, and reinstated Theodore Rshtuni. The death of Rshtuni in 654 A.D., combined with the crisis in the caliphate and the eventual Sunni-Shi'i split, presented the Byzantines with a perfect opportunity to put the Mamikonians back in power. Catholicos Nerses returned as well and quickly completed the construction of the church of Zvartnots. But by 661 A.D., the struggle for the caliphate was over. The Umayyad family, led by Ma'wiyah, had defeated 'Ali and his followers (the Shi'a) and had established a dynasty. The Umayyads now forced the catholicos and the Mamikonians to accept Arab suzerainty and to pay an annual tribute in gold in exchange for governing Armenia.

The Byzantines renewed the pressure to subjugate Armenia politically and ecclesiastically. Justinian II and his Khazar allies even invaded

Armenia in the late seventh century but were defeated by the Armeno-
Arab force. The Arabs had yet not began to settle in Armenia, which
remained autonomous for the time being. The Armenians built churches
and fortresses, agriculture expanded, and trade increased substantially.
Political power alternated between the Mamikonian and the Bagratuni
families under Arab suzerainty, while the remaining *nakharars* continued
to control their ancestral lands. Contrary to popular belief, there was no
religious persecution by the Muslims during this period. The catholicos
was free to travel and maintain his jurisdiction over the Caucasian
Albanian Church, which had tried unsuccessfully to follow the example
of the Georgians and unite with the Greek Church.

This peace and prosperity ended in the eighth century. The later
Umayyads, and especially their successors, the 'Abbasids, created large
empires which required additional taxes. Taxes were increased throughout the Arab empire, and centralized control tightened considerably in
order to collect them. Continued Khazar and Byzantine incursions into
Armenia made it obvious that Armenian leaders could not effectively
defend the Armenian borders of the Arab empire. Armenia was becoming
a burden for the Umayyads, who, as stipulated in the agreement of 652
A.D., had to pay for the maintenance of the Armenian cavalry. Direct
rule there would guarantee greater control and more taxes. In 701 A.D.,
therefore, the Umayyad caliph began the formal annexation of Armenia
by sending his brother at the head of a large force.

Both the Byzantines and the Arabs reorganized the Armenian lands
under their control. The Byzantines, having lost their domains in Greater
Armenia, replaced First and Second Armenia with military districts called
themes, the main one of which was called Armeniakon. Each *theme* was
headed by a general in charge of civil and military affairs. Troops were
recruited locally and were given land in return for their military service.
The land could not be sold but, in turn, passed to their sons, who assumed
responsibility for military duty. Eventually these *themes* were broken up
into smaller ones and remained under the control of Byzantine military
governors until the arrival of the Turks. The Umayyads created the
province of "al-Arminiya," which included most of Greater Armenia,
eastern Georgia, and Caucasian Albania (see map 14). Dvin served as
the capital of the region and became the seat of the Muslim governor, or

ostikan. Arabs installed garrisons in the major cities while Armenian *nakharars* maintained their autonomy under the *ostikan*, with no single family gaining dominance. Islamic law was enforced in Armenia and a number of religious and secular leaders were taken to Damascus as hostages. By 703 A.D. the *nakharars*, unhappy with the repressive policies, had rebelled and solicited Byzantine help. The rebellion brought an even larger Arab force, which spared the Church, but decimated the ranks of the *nakharars* in a massacre at Nakhichevan.

By 705 A.D. the Umayyads, attacked by the Khazars and facing a disgruntled non-Arab Muslim population at home, had eased restrictions and once again permitted the Armenians a degree of autonomy. Some of the *nakharars* fought with the Arabs against the Khazars, and the next two decades was a period of close cooperation between the Arabs and Armenians. The Arabs were particularly lenient toward the Church, which had not participated in the rebellion and which, according to Islamic law, was viewed as the primary leader of the Armenians. This climate enabled the Church, for the first time, to organize the collection of its canons, a milestone in Armenian Church history.

A primary motivation for the collection of the canons was probably the emergence of the Paulician heresy. The Paulician heresy began in the late sixth century, but gained momentum in the seventh century after the rise of Islam and the weakening of the power of established Churches. The Paulicians were the successors to the early Christian and Manichean non-conformists, who maintained a dualistic doctrine, that is the belief in the universally antagonistic forces of good and evil. The Paulicians were opposed to the traditional social values of the establishment. They were against procreation, eating meat, and holding property, and formed an underground movement which led armed attacks against Armenian, Arab, and Byzantine religious and secular authorities. By the end of the seventh century, the Paulician movement had spread into parts of Armenia, Persia, and northern Mesopotamia and posed a major threat to civil authorities. In 719 A.D. Catholicos John of Odzun, supported by the *nakharars* and the Arabs, convened a council at Dvin at which he publicly ordered the repression of the Paulicians. Similar decrees were enacted at another council in 726 A.D. The Paulicians eventually left Armenia and established a republic northwest of the Euphrates where they became a thorn in the side of Byzantium. The year 726 A.D. also witnessed the start of the century-long debate over icons in the Byzantine empire, a crisis which for a time freed the Armenian Church from further interference by the Greek Church.

The 'Abbasids and Armenia

In 750 A.D. an event took place in the Muslim world which brought in a new order and changed its relations with Armenia: the 'Abbasid revolution. Unlike the Umayyads, the 'Abbasids formed a truly Islamic, rather than simply an Arab, empire. Persians, Turks, and even Christian converts, as well as Arabs, could now hold high office. The capital was moved from the Arab center of Damascus to Baghdad, and the administration became more imperial. Fiscal demands increased taxation, which had already been on the rise during the late Umayyad period.

The Armenians took advantage of the confusion in Damascus, staged a minor rebellion, and sought aid from Byzantium against the Arabs. The rivalry between the Mamikonians and the Bagratunis, as well as Byzantium's iconoclastic controversy, thwarted the success of the uprising and the 'Abbasids soon re-established Arab control over Armenia. Neither the Bagratunis, viewed by the 'Abbasids as pro-Umayyad, nor the Mamikonians, viewed as pro-Byzantine, gained the immediate trust of the 'Abbasids. Reduction of trade, the virtual disappearance of silver, heavy taxes, and the maintenance of the Armenian cavalry, which now fell to the Armenians, forced some Armenian *nakharars*, like the Amatuni, to emigrate to Byzantium. By the third quarter of the eighth century, the Bagratunis, however, had managed to mend relations with the 'Abbasids and win their recognition as the leaders of the Armenians.

The Mamikonians, the Artsrunis, and the Byzantines were not pleased with this rapprochement and, in 774 A.D., incited a rebellion in Armenia in which a number of Arab tax collectors were killed. The Bagratunis cautioned the other *nakharars* against provoking Baghdad. Their advice was ignored, however, and an Armenian force was assembled to face the Arabs. The Armenian defeat at Bagrevand in 775 A.D. cost the lives of most of the ruling generation of *nakharars* and critically weakened a number of Armenian houses such as the Rshtuni, Gnuni, and the Mami-

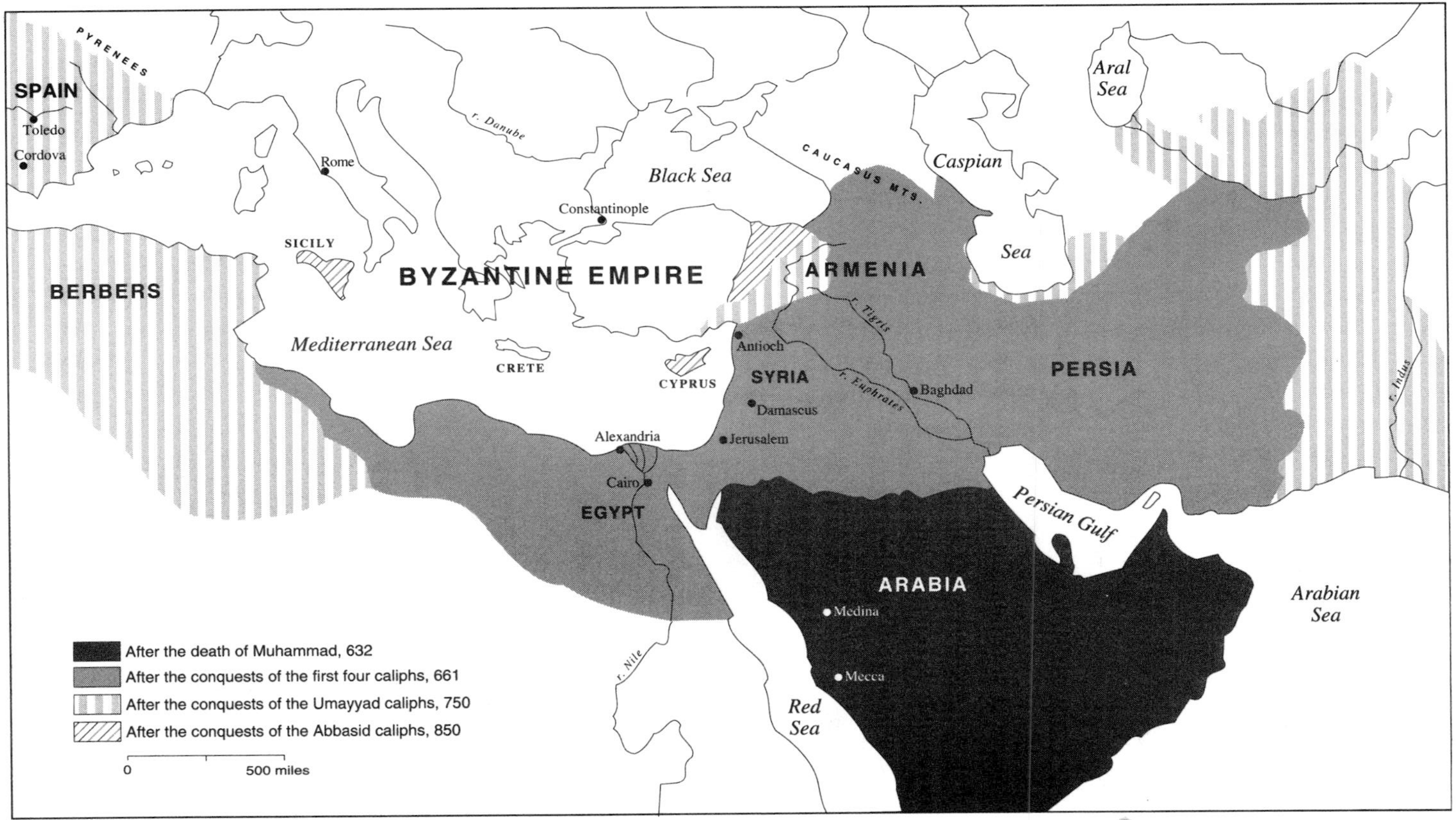
PYRENEES
SPAIN
Toledo
Cordova
Rome
r. Danube
Black Sea
CAUCASUS MTS.
Caspian
Sea
Aral
Sea
Constantinople
SICILY
BYZANTINE EMPIRE
BERBERS
ARMENIA
Mediterranean Sea
CRETE
CYPRUS
Antioch
SYRIA
r. Tigris
r. Euphrates
Baghdad
PERSIA
r. Indus
Damascus
Jerusalem
Alexandria
Cairo
EGYPT
Persian Gulf
ARABIA
Arabian
Sea
Medina
Mecca
r. Nile
Red
Sea
After the death of Muhammad, 632
After the conquests of the first four caliphs, 661
After the conquests of the Umayyad caliphs, 750
After the conquests of the Abbasid caliphs, 850
0
500 miles

14. The Expansion of Islam

konian families. In fact, this last never again played a significant role in the history of Armenia. The Bagratunis, on the other hand, retained their position as leaders of the Armenians.

The rule of Harun al-Rashid (786-809 A.D.), at the end of the eighth century, completed the consolidation of the 'Abbasid empire and signified another major change for Armenia and the Arab world. For the first time, Arab soldiers and merchants were actively encouraged to settle and establish new communities in Arab-held territories, including Armenia. Trade, especially, began to spread Islam to the coastal cities of Africa and south and southeast Asia. Baghdad appointed Arab families to rule in or colonize Armenia and other parts of Transcaucasia. Barda'a (Partav), Tiflis, Gandzak, Dvin, Nakhichevan, and Diyarbekir (Diyar-bakr) became Arab administrative centers, governed by emirs. Intermarriages and forced, as well as genuine, conversions took place, and some of the Arab clans, such as the Shaybani and Jahhaf, even assimilated into the ranks of the Armenian *nakharars*. The province of al-Arminiya was now divided into Arminiya, Georgia, and Arran (Caucasian Albania). The Arab emirs were no longer temporary governors or commanders of garrisons, but like the Kaysites, who settled near Lake Van, made parts of Armenia their new home. Fortunately for Armenia, these Arab emirates never included a majority of the population, nor were they united.

After the decline of the 'Abbasids in the ninth century, the emirates acted independently of Baghdad. The death of Harun al-Rashid began the long decline of the caliphate and the central Arab authority, the *ostikan*, was forced to move from Dvin to Barda'a on the easternmost corner of Armenia. This fragmentation of Arab authority provided the opportunity for the resurgence of Bagratuni leadership under Ashot Msaker ["the Meat-Eater"] (790-826 A.D.).

The Rise of the Bagratunis

At the start of the ninth century, Ashot expanded his domains at the expense of the weakening Mamikonians and Kamsarakans. He clashed with a number of independent emirs who had broken with the caliph and was rewarded by Baghdad with the title of prince of Armenia. His uncle established the Bagratuni house of Iberia (Georgia). Upon Ashot's death in 826 A.D., his oldest son, Bagrat, assumed the title of prince of princes, while his younger son was named *sparapet*. In the meantime, in Vaspurakan, the Artsrunis were also creating a power base. The princes of Siunik made a marriage alliance with Babak, a Mazdakite Persian, who in 816 A.D. had rebelled against Baghdad and had established himself in parts of Artsakh between Arran and Azerbaijan. It is important to note that some Armenian houses allied themselves with Muslims against Baghdad or even other Armenians. The same was true of the Muslims, who would occasionally ally with Armenians against other Muslims. In Baghdad there was internal strife over the succession between al-Ma'mun, the son of a Persian wife of Harun, and al-Amin, the son of a Turkish wife. Al-Ma'mun was eventually the victor and was succeeded by his brother, al-Mu'tasim.

In 836 A.D. Afshin, a Muslim Persian general, was sent by al-Mu'tasim to capture Babak. Afshin promised the Armenians and the Persians a degree of autonomy and tax remissions if they cooperated against Babak. Babak was betrayed and captured one year later. A number of his followers then gathered around another leader, Mazyar, and started a social revolution against the Islamicized land-owners of the Caspian region. Afshin, who had gained influence in Azerbaijan, was accused of backing the rebels and in 841 A.D., was killed by the caliph. Eventually a new commander was appointed in Azerbaijan from the Sajids, a family which would have a major impact on Armenia. It is at this time that social unrest in Persia spread into Armenia with the appearance of a group of heretics known as the Tondrakians. The Tondrakians appear to have been either remnants of the Paulicians, who had fled Byzantine persecutions after the fall of their republic, followers of Babak, or lower classes of society influenced by either group.

In the meantime, al-Mu'tasim had begun to employ Turkish slaves and mercenaries for his main army. As with the largely German Praetorian Guard who assumed increasing power in Rome, this policy resulted in the domination of the caliphate by the Turks, until the arrival of the Persian Buyids in the early tenth century. Rivalry among Turkish, Arab, and Persian factions forced al-Mu'tasim, in 836 A.D., to move the capital north to Samarra on the Tigris' eastern bank, where it remained until 870 A.D. In 847 A.D. the Turks installed al-Mutawakkil as the new caliph at Samarra. The new caliph employed the most severe measures to restore the power of the caliphate. The translation of Greek philosophical works were halted, and Jews and Christians were persecuted.

It is against this backdrop that a second major rebellion in Armenia occurred in 850-851 A.D., this time against al-Mutawakkil's taxes and repressive policies. A new *ostikan* was sent to Armenia but was refused entry. Instead Bagrat Bagratuni, the son of Ashot Msaker, sent an embassy with the required taxes to the caliph himself, signifying that, although vassals of the caliph, Armenia would keep its autonomous status. The caliph viewed this act as rebellion. The *ostikan's* army invaded Armenia but was defeated by Bagrat, who had allied himself with the Artsrunis of Vaspurakan. The caliph then sent a new army. The Artsrunis sent gifts which were delivered by the mother of the *nakharar* of Vaspurakan, Lady Hripsimé, who succeeded in halting the Arab attack on her domains. Bagrat had to fight alone and was soon captured and sent to Samarra where he was killed (852 A.D.). The Armenian population then rose up and killed the Arab general, forcing the Arab army out of Bagratuni domains in Taron. The rebellion united most of the *nakharars* against the Muslims. The caliph sent a large army to crush the rebellion and to subdue all the *nakharars* once and for all. Smbat Bagratuni, the brother of Bagrat and the *sparapet*, refused to join the rebels, possibly to signal the caliph that, as the new leader of the Armenians, he was a loyal subject and willing to compromise. Mutawakkil would accept no compromises, however. The Arab army, under the command of the Turkish general Bugha, ravaged Armenia, Georgia and Caucasian Albania. By 853 A.D. Bugha had captured most of the important *nakharars*, including Smbat Bagratuni, and brought them to Samarra. All of the *nakharars*, with the exception of Smbat, in order to save their lives, agreed to apostatize and were allowed to return home after the death of Mutawakkil. Smbat alone remained in Samarra where he died.

Mutawakkil's campaigns were the last attempt of the caliphate at direct control of Armenia. His murder at the hands of his Turkish troops in 861 A.D. hastened the decline of the 'Abbasids. During the captivity of the *nakharars*, the Arab emirs were free to expand. At the same time, Byzantium had finally revived under Basil I (867-886 A.D.) of the Macedonian dynasty. After their return, the *nakharars*, especially the

Bagratuni and Artsruni, continued their struggle against the Arab emirs. The major clashes occurred in the southern regions, mainly in Taron, Sasun, Vaspurakan, and Mokk, with the Armenians holding their own against the Arabs.

Arts, Literature, Architecture

The two most important Armenian histories of this period are by Bishop Sebeos and Ghevond. Sebeos provides valuable information on Byzantium and Persia in the late sixth and early seventh centuries. He then describes the birth of Islam and the Arab invasions of Persia, Armenia, and the Byzantine empire to 661 A.D. Ghevond's history details the Arab domination of Armenia from 661 to 788 A.D. One result of the Armeno-Arab struggles of this period was the birth of the popular oral epic the *Daredevils of Sasun* and its hero, David of Sasun. The story, which was recorded centuries later, depicts the Bagratunis, led by David, the Rshtunis, in the figure of uncle Toros, and Msr-melik, who represents the Muslim leader. Bugha and the Arstrunis are also represented. The victory of David against the stronger forces of the Arabs, represents a sort of David and Goliath struggle between good and evil.

In the field of architecture, the church of Zvartnots (644-652 A.D.) is a perfect example of a niche buttressed square with four lobes, known as a quatrefoil. Unlike other such structures, Zvartnots had a circular ambulatory with a square chamber outside the circle. Although the church was destroyed in the tenth century, its remains are the primary examples of the sculpture of this period in the form of reliefs of the workers and planners of the structure. In the field of painting, an illustrated Gospel, dated 862 A.D. and commissioned by the Artsruni family, is noteworthy for its highly stylized manner.

By the late ninth century, following more than two centuries of Arab incursions, Armenians still formed the majority of the population, and the Arab emirs had difficulty maintaining their holdings in Armenia. The many mountains and valleys of Armenia controlled by regional *nakharars* served as multiple havens of Armenian autonomy. The son of Smbat, Ashot Bagratuni, became the rallying force and continued to exert pressure on the Arab emirs. The prestige of the Bagratunis was on the rise within Armenia and both the weakened caliphate and the emerging Macedonian dynasty in Byzantium realized the value of an Armenian alliance. Conditions were, therefore, right for the emergence of a new Armenian kingdom.

C.E.	ARMENIA & GEORGIA	ISLAMIC MIDDLE EAST	BYZANTIUM & THE WEST	INDIA, CHINA & JAPAN	SUB-SAHARAN AFRICA & THE AMERICAS
900	Artsrunis receive crown from Yusuf (908)	Rise of Sufism	Cluny founded (910)	Five Dynasties in China (907-960)	Kingdom of Ghana (c. 900-1100)
	Ashot II (The Iron) (914-929)	al-Muktafi (902-908)	Reconquista begins in Spain (910)	Wood-block printing widespread in China and Japan	Toltec Empire in Tula, Mexico (c. 900-1200)
	Abas (929-953)	Yusuf (c. 906-929) rules Azerbaijan	Otto I (The Great) (936-973)	Sung Dynasty (960-1279)	Collapse of Mayan civilization
	Ashot III (953-977)	Sallarids (c. 916-1090)	Russian state founded in Kiev (c. 950)		
	Ani becomes capital of Armenia	Rawwadids (c. 920-1071)	Basil II (976-1025)		
		Buyids (932-1062)	Byzantines convert Russians (988)		
	Smbat II (977-990)	al-Farabi (d. 950)	Capetian dynasty in France (989)		
		Shaddadids (c. 951-1174)			
	Gagik I (990-1020)	Ghaznavids (962-1186)			
		Fatimids in Egypt (c. 968-1171) al-Azhar university in Cairo			
1000			Romanesque architecture (c. 1000-1200)		Kingdom of Kanen in Africa
					Islam penetrates sub-Saharan and East Africa
	King of Vaspurakan wills his kingdom to Byzantium (1022)			Turks and Afghans conquer northern India (1022)	Incas settle in Cuzco Valley in Andes
	Hovhannes Smbat (1020-1042)	Avicenna (d. 1037)		Feudalism in Japan, code of Bushido	
	Gagik II (1042-1045)	Seljuks (c. 1038-1194)	Split of Roman and Greek Churches (1054)	Tale of Genji	
	Fall of Ani—end of Bagratunis of Ani (1045)		Normans conquer England (1066)	Vietnam independent from China	
	Fall of Kars—end of Bagratunis of Kars (1064)	Seljuks in Baghdad (1055)	Pope Gregory VII (1073-1085)		
	Large Armenian emigration to Byzantium and Cilicia	Danishmandids (1071-1177)	Struggle between Church and State in the West (1073-1122)		
	Rise of Rubenid and Hetumid houses in Cilicia (c. 1070-1085)	Battle of Manzikert (1071)	Seljuks of Rum (1077-1307)		
	Rise of Zakarids in Armenia and Georgia	Assassins in Alamut (1090)	Peter Abelard (1079-1142)		
	David the Builder of Georgia (1089-1125)	First Crusade (1096-1099)	St. Bernard of Clairvaux (1090-1153)		
		Crusaders conquer Jerusalem (1099)	Crusade preached by Pope Urban II (1095)		
			Comneni emperors (1081-1185)		

Table 8: 900 A.D. to 1100 A.D.

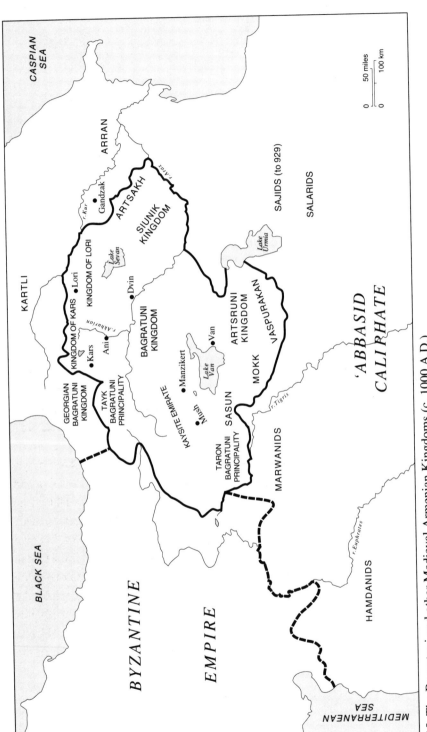

15. The Bagratuni and other Medieval Armenian Kingdoms (c. 1000 A.D.)

IX

A Land of Many Crowns:

The Bagratuni (Bagratid) Dynasty and the Armenian Medieval Kingdoms (884-1045 A.D.)

The almost two centuries of Bagratuni rule in parts of Greater Armenia coincided with the time when the Carolingian empire disintegrated, and separate states began to form in England, France, and Germany. Romanesque architecture was developing, and the monastic reforms initiated at Cluny made monasteries vital centers of religious and intellectual life. Europe experienced the height of the Viking raids. The *reconquista* began in Spain, while the Normans conquered England. The Greek Orthodox and Roman Catholic Churches split. Japan and China began the woodblock printing of books. The Sung dynasty ruled in China and in Japan the *bushido* code brought forth the samurai. The world's first reputed novel, *The Tale of Genji*, was written by Lady Murasaki. Arab and Persian science reached its zenith with Avecinna. Sufism became a major literary and religious force in the Middle East. The first Russian state was founded in Kiev and was soon after converted to Christianity by the Byzantines. Islam penetrated sub-Saharan Africa, while the kingdoms of Ghana and Kanem emerged there as well. The Muslims conquered northern India. The Incas settled in the Cuzco valley of Peru, the classical Mayan civilization collapsed, and the Toltecs replaced the Olmecs in Mexico.

The Revival of the Armenian Kingdom

In the last half of the ninth century, Armenia was experiencing a power vacuum. The Byzantines and the 'Abbasids were too preoccupied with internal and external affairs to focus their attention on Armenia, but there were few *nakharar* houses strong enough to take advantage of the situation. Some had left Armenia, others had died out or were weakened by their own internal feuds. The apostasy of the *nakharars* at Samarra, and their eight-year absence from Armenia, further weakened the political structure.

Into this vacuum stepped Ashot Bagratuni, the son of Smbat, who had died at Samarra. Immediately upon his father's death, he assumed the title of *tanuter* and *sparapet* of the Bagratuni house, and became the rallying point for Armenian resistance against Arab domination.

Ashot was soon able to increase both Bagratuni power and prestige. Between 855 and 862 A.D. he expanded his domains by annexing both the Mamikonian and Kamsarakan holdings and through marriage alliances with the Bagratunis of Georgia and the Artsrunis of Vaspurakan. Thus, the northern, southern, and western parts of Greater Armenia were either controlled by or allied with the Bagratunis. In addition, Ashot made a point of maintaining friendly relations with the lords of Siunik in the east. With the residence of the catholicos within his borders, Ashot also enjoyed the critical support of the Church.

Ashot and the later Bagratunis faced several internal and external obstacles, however, which prevented them from ever reunifying Greater Armenia. The first were the Siunis and the Artsrunis, the only other *nakharar* houses of any strength left in Armenia, who often withheld their support or actively allied against the Bagratunis. The second, and more immediate, internal impediment was the Arab *ostikan* and the Arab emirates. The *ostikan* alternated his residence between Barda'a and Dvin, thus driving a wedge between the Bagratunis on one side and Georgia and Siunik on the other. The emirates occupied the central lands of Greater Armenia between the Bagratunis and Artsrunis. Ashot and his successors were thus never able to link Armenian-held lands into a united front against the Arabs. Moreover, the important cities of Dvin and

Nakhichevan, among others, remained under Arab control for most of the period.

External forces posed a more overt threat to the Bagratunis. With the start of the Macedonian dynasty in Byzantium in 867 A.D., Constantinople once again began to play an intrusive role in the affairs of Armenia. Their common Christianity — and, in the case of the Macedonian emperors, common Armenian ancestry — did little to foster a strong Armeno-Byzantine alliance against the Arabs. Rather, the Byzantines maintained their policy of demanding theological concessions and control of Armenian lands in return for military aid. The steady decline of the 'Abbasid caliphate allowed the rise of minor Muslim dynasties on the southern and southeastern borders of Armenia and periodically threatened its security.

Although he transferred his title of *sparapet* to his younger brother, there is little doubt that Ashot maintained full control over the *nakharar* army, which at that time still had some semblance of unity. To further secure his position, Ashot renewed the alliance with Byzantium and, at least officially, approved of a dialogue on Greek Orthodox and Armenian Church unity. The 'Abbasid caliph al-Musta'in saw in the growing power of the Bagratunis a possible check to the increasing independence of the Arab emirates. In 862 A.D. he conferred on Ashot the title of prince of princes and, according to some historians, the power to levy taxes. Although the title may have included suzerainty over Georgia and other parts of the Caucasus, the presence of the *ostikan* in Barda'a meant that, in all probability, Ashot's rule never extended beyond parts of Greater Armenia. The Armenian Church, supported by Ashot, once again assumed jurisdiction over the Caucasian Albanian Church. Ashot was already acknowledged as ruler of Armenia by most of the *nakharars* and the Church when, in 884 A.D., the caliph al-Mu'tamid sent him a royal crown and Ashot, the fifth Bagratuni prince to bear that name, was crowned King Ashot I. Shortly after, the Byzantine emperor, Basil I, sent a crown as well, to maintain his influence with the new dynasty. For the moment, Armenia once more possessed a kingdom and a dynasty. During the next six years Ashot not only extended his political influence over the emirates, but enabled the Georgian Bagratunis to consolidate their control in Iberia (see map 15). Ashot gained control of Dvin but did not move his court there, preferring to remain in his stronghold at Bagaran. This decision was not without serious consequences, for it periodically left Dvin and the center of Armenia unprotected and, at times, in Arab hands.

Ashot's death in 890 A.D. immediately revealed a number of problems which were to plague the Bagratunis. The five hundred years of partitions and decentralization had resulted in political fragmentation and the loss of a framework for a single state. Furthermore, the large *nakharar* houses had since the sixth century broken up into smaller branches which fought among themselves. In addition, the Siunik lands in the east were separated from the Artsruni territories in the south by Nakhichevan and the Arax valley which were in the hands of Muslim emirs. Dvin, Tiflis, Nakhichevan, and other cities in the center thus continued to remain under Arab control. Moreover, the emirs never united nor always obeyed the 'Abbasid caliphs, a situation which at times aided, and at others, hurt the Armenians and the Bagratunis.

After Ashot's death, his son, Smbat I (890-914 A.D.), assumed the throne and immediately faced many of the same internal and external problems as had his father. Lacking the personal authority of his father, Smbat could not totally command the Church or the *nakharars*, particularly the Artsrunis; even his uncle refused to recognize his nephew. The Artsrunis, stating that in the past the Bagratunis had been no more than the traditional coronants of the Arshakuni monarchs, now questioned the legitimacy of the Bagratunis as kings. In the early part of his rule, however, Smbat managed to keep the support of Byzantium, his Georgian relatives, and the catholicos, as well as Mohammad, the Sajid ruler of Azerbaijan and the *ostikan.*

Rival Kingdoms in Armenia

The latter part of Smbat's rule was a failure. Mohammad attacked Armenia, Dvin and Nakhichevan were taken and the catholicos captured. Smbat managed to conclude a peace agreement with Mohammad and ransom the catholicos, who left for the Holy See in Dvin, which was now in Muslim hands. Although Caucasian Albania remained loyal, Siunik and the Artsrunis at Vaspurakan made a number of friendly overtures to Mohammad. The latter took advantage of the situation to invade Armenia once again. Smbat's wife and the royal treasury were captured. In exchange for his wife's release, Smbat was forced to sent his eldest son Ashot as hostage, to give his niece as one of Mohammad's wives, and to pay tribute to Mohammad's son, the governor of Dvin. Mohammad then attacked Vaspurakan and made the Artsrunis his vassals, taking the brother of the *nakharar* as hostage.

The situation improved for a brief period when the caliph al-Muktafi, fearing Sajid power, released Armenia from Sajid control. The Siunik and Vaspurakan leaders then quickly renewed their allegiance to the Bagratunis. The picture changed radically, however, when Mohammad's brother, Yusuf, became the *ostikan* in 901 A.D. Taking advantage of the death of Mohammad, Smbat requested direct vassalage to the caliph thus bypassing the *ostikan*. Yusuf ignored the caliph's supremacy and invaded Bagratuni territory. Baghdad's inaction resulted in an agreement in 903 A.D., by which Smbat accepted Yusuf's authority and received a crown for his submission. Smbat's position weakened further when he involved himself in a dispute between a Georgian prince and the Bagratuni king of Georgia, and in another dispute between the Siunis and the Artsrunis, alienating both houses. Taking advantage of the division among the Christians, Yusuf demanded additional taxes beyond the tribute paid by Smbat to Baghdad. To weaken Smbat further, Yusuf in 908 A.D. granted a crown to Gagik Artsruni, creating an autonomous kingdom in the south. Bagratuni Armenia was on the road to fragmentation. A year later, the combined Muslim and Artsruni forces attacked Smbat's territory and wreaked havoc on the land. Smbat sought aid from Byzantium and the caliph, but both were distracted by domestic problems. Yusuf captured and killed Armenian princes, including a son and a nephew of Smbat. To stop the bloodshed, Smbat surrendered, and was tortured and crucified.

Smbat's death served a purpose, however. The cruelty of Yusuf towards Smbat and other *nakharars* cost him the support of Gagik Artsruni and other Armenian leaders who now joined Smbat's son Ashot II, known as *Erkat* (Iron), and drove the Muslims out of most of Greater Armenia. The Georgian Bagratunis also came back to the fold, and Ashot II was crowned in 914 A.D. Ashot's cousin, however, remained loyal to Yusuf, who installed him as governor of Dvin. Immediately thereafter, the Byzantines, who were troubled by the events in Armenia, offered their assistance in removing the Muslim threat for good. Ashot II went to Constantinople where a Christian union against the common enemy was discussed. In 915 A.D. Ashot returned with a Byzantine army, and although he was unable to take Dvin, he extended his influence considerably. Yusuf's rebellion against the caliph and his arrest in 919 A.D. removed the most dangerous Bagratuni foe and at the same time ended the autonomy of Ashot's cousin in Dvin. Gagik Artsruni in Vaspurakan and Ashot II began an era of reconstruction and rebuilding in Greater Armenia.

As noted, a major problem for the Bagratunis was the attitude of Byzantium, which occasionally gave aid but demanded political and religious submission in return. Ashot II was not spared. No sooner had he mended his relations with the new *ostikan* than the Byzantines dispatched forces to destabilize Armenia. In the meantime Yusuf was released from jail, resumed his position of *ostikan*, and began new attacks on his immediate neighbors, Siunik and Vaspurakan. Ashot and his loyal *nakharars* managed to defeat both the Arabs and the Greeks. The last years of Ashot's rule were peaceful. Ironically, both Ashot and Yusuf died in 929 A.D., and a new era began for Armenia when the Sajid interlude in Azerbaijan ended.

Ashot's brother Abas assumed the leadership of the Bagratunis in 929 A.D. and ruled until 953 A.D. The rise of the various Kurdo-Iranian dynasties in Azerbaijan and parts of Armenia, such as the Rawaddids, combined with the constant threat from Byzantium and the Arab emirs in Mesopotamia, kept Abas busy. He chose to stay in his own domains and strengthen his defenses from his capital, the fortress of Kars. Gagik of Vaspurakan remained the most powerful Armenian force. A number of catholicoses were chosen by him and stayed at his court, mainly because Dvin remained in Muslim hands. Vaspurakan became a major political and cultural center and the island of Aghtamar in Lake Van became the Holy See of Armenia. By the mid-tenth century, thanks to Gagik's efforts, Armenia had restored much of its former political and economic position.

The reign of Ashot III (953-977 A.D.) began the seventy-year apex of Bagratuni rule. Following the death of Gagik of Vaspurakan, Ashot became the undisputed leader of the Armenians. The catholicos came to Ashot's new capital at Ani and crowned him king. Ashot, in turn, supported the Church and sponsored many new edifices. Ashot made sure that the Caucasian Albanian Church once again accepted the authority of the Armenian Church. He also managed to capture Dvin. Armenia was relatively powerful and united, and when the Byzantine emperor, John Tzimiskes, arrived with an army in 974 A.D., he was forced to withdraw. Ashot felt so secure that he granted his brother the fortress of Kars and permitted him to use the title of king. He also gave the region north of Lake Sevan to his son, who soon assumed the title of King of Lori. This pattern was unfortunately repeated in Vaspurakan, which was divided among the heirs of Gagik. By the last quarter of the tenth century Siunik had also become a kingdom (see map 15). Such proliferation of titles and crowns posed little danger provided that strong rulers controlled Armenia from Ani. In fact, the granting of titles may have stopped squabbles and given power to those who otherwise might have plotted against the kingdom, allied with enemies, or rebelled after the death of the king. Problems arose, of course, during the reigns of weak kings or when outside pressures became overwhelming. In addition, bishops in these "kingdoms" occasionally chose to ignore the central authority of the Church and styled themselves as catholicoses.

Following the death of Ashot III, his son, Smbat II, assumed the throne and had to deal with his uncle at Kars and the Muslims. Dvin once again changed hands, but Smbat spent his years expanding the city of Ani, which became a major urban center with a cathedral and many churches. With the help of the Georgian Bagratunis, Smbat reconciled with his uncle and assumed the leadership of the Armenian Bagratunis. The rivalry among the Muslim emirs enabled Smbat to resist Muslim advances and to expand his domains.

Gagik I Bagratuni, not to be confused with Gagik of Vaspurakan, assumed the throne in 990 A.D. Vaspurakan was too fragmented to challenge him, and Gagik enjoyed the support or submission of all his clan who ruled in various parts of Armenia, as well as other *nakharars*. Unfortunately Byzantium, under Basil II, took control of western Georgia and was thus close enough to Armenia to cause future intrigue.

The Fall of the Bagratunis

The death of Gagik in 1020 A.D. began the rapid decline and collapse of the Bagratunis. The potential forces for the destruction of the kingdom were all present long before, but had been kept in check by the authority of strong Bagratuni rulers. The rivalry between Gagik's sons resulted in the partitioning of the kingdom. All this came at a time when the Turks appeared on the scene, and Basil II was extending his empire by annexing weaker neighbors. The Byzantines had already taken southwestern Armenia when, in 1022 A.D., the old king of Vaspurakan, Senekerim, exchanged his kingdom for lands in Byzantium. The Bagratuni king of Ani, Hovhannes-Smbat, feeling insecure, and childless, left his kingdom to Basil. After his death in 1042 A.D., the pro-Byzantine faction tried to hand the city over but Prince Gagik II and his supporters resisted and Ani remained independent. Gagik ruled for three years during which he was attacked by the emir of Dvin, the Byzantines, and his kinsmen from Lori. He went to Constantinople to plead his case but was forced to abdicate. Thus, in 1045 A.D., the last major Armenian kingdom in historic Armenia came to an end. The Byzantines took Ani, and by 1064 A.D. the Bagratuni kingdom of Kars had also been annexed. Only two mountainous kingdoms and a principality remained autonomous: the kingdom of Siunik, to 1166, the kingdom of Lori, to c. 1100, and the principality of Khachen, to c. 1450.

Armenians in the Byzantine Empire

Armenians had settled in the eastern parts of the Roman empire prior to the Christian era and had risen to prominent positions. Even the Emperor Heraclius is reputed to have been from Armenian descent. Although Justinian began forcibly transplanting Armenian families to Byzantium, their numbers were very few. Armenians began to enter Byzantium in large numbers in the late sixth century, when Red Vardan Mamikonian, together with his followers, and the Catholicos John II, fled to Constantinople after the unsuccessful rebellion against the Sasanids. Vardan and his retinue reportedly entered the Byzantine army and settled in Pergamum. The reign of Maurice and the second partition of Armenia forcefully removed thousands of Armenians to the Byzantine empire, a large group of whom settled in Cyprus. In the second half of the seventh century, Armenian Paulicians, driven from their homes in Armenia, settled in Byzantine territory, mainly in Pontus. After the Arab invasions and until the tenth century, more Armenians *nakharars* with their entire families migrated to Byzantium, some settling in Cilicia. The decline and fall of the Bagratuni kingdom in the eleventh century brought more *nakharars* to Cilicia, as well as Constantinople and other urban centers of the empire. More would arrive following the later Turko-Mongol invasions, and they remained an important commercial and administrative force in Constantinople following the fall of Byzantium to the Turks.

Historians consider the Armenians as one of the most influential groups in the multi-national Byzantine empire. Armenians engaged in trade, administration and farming and they were a dominant element in the army. There were sixteen generals in Justinian's army alone whose Armenian contingents were known for their valor. A number of Armenian military leaders became provincial governors, while others became the power behind the throne and were instrumental in elevating a number of emperors. The Macedonian dynasty, which according to a number of Byzantinists, was of Armenian origin, is considered the apex of Armenian dominance in the political and military structure of the empire. Starting with Basil I in 867 A.D. and ending with the death of Basil II in 1025 A.D., the Armenians emperors, generals, and military contingents had their greatest military successes against the Arabs, the Slavs, and Bulgars. Ironically, it was this same Armenian dynasty which was chiefly responsible for the breakup of the Bagratuni kingdom; however, as will be seen in the next chapter, they were also indirectly responsible for the rise of a new Armenia in Cilicia.

Trade, Art, Architecture and Learning:

The Bagratuni kings did not mint any coins, and 'Abbasid and Byzantine coins were widely used in Armenia. Armenia at this time exported manufactured goods, silver, copper, iron, arsenic, borax, and salt. Dried fish was exported to Mesopotamia. Falcons were sent as tribute to the caliph, and Armenian horses and mules were highly prized. Armenia had forests, and walnut wood was exported to Baghdad, as were furs and leather goods. Armenian carpets were also in demand at this period, especially those made from goat hair. The textile industry thrived, mainly due to Armenian dyes. The wine-red dye, referred to by the Arabs as *kirmiz*, had been especially valued since antiquity, and was made from the dried shells of the cochineal, an insect which feeds on roots of a particular plant growing on the slopes of Mount Ararat. In addition, Armenia grew silk in the Artsakh, Siuni, and Gandzak regions.

The Bagratuni era produced a number of historians. Aristakes Lastivertsi described Armeno-Byzantine relations and the Tondrakian movement of the later Bagratuni period, ending his history with a detailed account of the Seljuk invasion of Ani and the Battle of Manzikert. John Mamikonian's *History of Taron* was written in the style of a medieval romance and focuses on the history of the House of the Mamikonians. Catholicos John Draskhanakertetsi (Catholicos Hovhannes V, known as the "historian") wrote a *History of Armenia* during this period. One of the most valuable works of this period, due to the accuracy of its chronology, is Stephen of Taron's (Stepan Taronetsi, also known as Asoghik) *History*. Thomas Artsruni's *History of the House of the Artsrunik* details conditions in Vaspurakan during the reign of King Gagik Artsruni. Movses Daskhurantsi's *The History of the Caucasian Albanians* is the only existing source in any language on this people, who were eventually assimilated by Armenians, Persians, Arabs, and Turks.

The Bagratuni period was the most prolific era of Armenian church architecture. In fact, most of the surviving churches in present-day Armenia are from this period. The Bagratuni kings, wealthy merchants, and *nakharars* supported the construction of numerous of churches in Ani, some of which have survived. The churches on Lake Sevan and the cathedrals of Kars, Argina, and Ani, as well as the monasteries of Marmashen and Khdskunk, were completed. The construction of the monasteries of Tatev, Sanahin, Haghpat, Geghard, and Makaravank began in this period and continued for the next two centuries. The castle-fortress and church of Amberd and the church of Bdjni are also from this period. One of the most impressive architectural monuments

is the Cathedral of Holy Cross in Aghtamar, commissioned by Gagik King
Artsruni. This jewel of architecture and relief sculpture contains impressive wall paintings representing Adam and Eve, the Annunciation, and the Last Judgement. Other masterpieces of relief sculpture are represented in the numerous *khachkars*, or stone-lace crosses, which began to appear in the ninth century and would reach their zenith in the fourteenth century.

The illuminated manuscripts of this period represent a number of schools. They either stress the decoration at the expense of the human form, or emphasize the natural appearance of the human form, as illustrated in the Edjmiadsin Gospel of 989 A.D. The most unique example of manuscript illumination is the Gospel of Moghni, which, using various styles of past and contemporary artists, arrived at a distinct Armenian style. By the eleventh century, Byzantine influence had begun to make inroads in a number of larger miniatures commissioned by the Bagratunis, as seen in the Trebizond Gospel at the Mkhitarist Library in Venice and the Gospel of King Gagik of Kars.

The Bagratunis, who claimed lineage from the Biblical King David and who occassionally wore turbans and adopted Arab names, restored the Armenian kingdom and, for a time, managed to balance Arab, Byzantine, and internal Armenian pressures. It was the unrelenting intrusive policy of the Byzantines, however, which finally destroyed the Bagratunis, as well as the Artsrunis. Ironically, Byzantium's policy toward Armenia contributed to the doom of its own empire, for with the with the Armenian buffer zone gone, and the Byzantines unable to replace the Armenian armies, the way was left open for the Seljuk Turks (see chapter XI). Ani fell in 1064 A.D. and Kars followed a year later. Finally, in 1071 A.D., the Seljuks defeated the Byzantine emperor in Manzikert and all of Armenia fell under Turkish rule. The Georgian Bagratunis, however, continued to flourish and ruled until the nineteenth century.

C.E.	(Historic and Cilicia) ARMENIA	ISLAMIC MIDDLE EAST & BYZANTIUM	EUROPE	INDIA, CHINA & JAPAN	SUB-SAHARAN AFRICA & THE AMERICAS
1100	Zakarids rule parts of Armenia as Georgian vassals (c. 1100-1236)	al-Ghazali (d. 1111)	Revival of towns and trade in the West (c. 1100-1300)	Angkor Wat in Kampuchea (c.1100- 1150)	Kingdom of Benin (1100-1897)
	Toros I (1102-1129)	Omar Khayyam (d. 1123)	Rise of universities in the West (c. 1100-1300)	China divided between Sung and Chin Dynasties (1127)	Post-Classical Mayan civilization at Chichen Itza, Central America
			Troubadour poetry in the West (c. 1100-1220)	Neo-Confucianism (c. 1130-1200)	
	Levon I (1129-1137)	Zangids (c. 1127-1222)	Henry I (England) (1100-1135)	Explosive powder used in China (c. 1150)	
			Louis IV (France) (1108-1137)		
	Toros II (1144-1169)	Second Crusade (1147-1149)	Concordat of Worms (1122)	Genghis Khan in Mongolia and China (c. 1162-1227)	
	Mleh (1170-1175)		Height of Cistercian monasticism (c. 1115-1153)		
	Ruben II (1175-1187)	Ayyubids in Egypt (1169-1250)	Aristotle translated into Latin (c. 1140-1260)		
			Gothic architecture (c. 1150-1500)	Kamakuro Shogunate in Japan (1185-1333)	
	Queen Tamar of Georgia (1184-1213)	Third Crusade (1189-1192)	Frederick I Barbarossa (Germany) (1152-1190)		
	Levon II (1187-1199) as King Levon I (1199-1219)	Sa 'di (1193-1292)	Henry II (England) (1154-1189)	Destruction of Buddhism in India (1192)	
		Averroes (d. 1198)	Thomas `a Becket (d. 1170)		
			Philip Augustus (France) (1180-1223)		
			Windmills invented (c. 1180)		
			Pope Innocent III (1198-1216)		
1200	Zabel (1219-1223)	Maimonides (d. 1204)	Albigensian Crusade (1208-1213)	Peak of Khmer Empire (c. 1200)	Kingdom of Mali (c. 1200-1450)
	Zabel and Philip (1223-1225)	Fourth Crusade (1202-1204)	Franciscan order founded (c. 1210)	Zen Buddhism in Japan (c. 1200)	
	Zabel and Hetum (1226-1269)	Fifth Crusade (1218-1221)	Roger Bacon (c. 1214-1294)	Small-pox innoculation in China (c.1200)	Decline of Ghana (c. 1224)
			Magna Carta (1215)	Sultanate of Delhi (1206-1526)	
	Mongols in Armenia (1236-1245)	Mamluks in Egypt (1250-1517)	Fourth Lateran Council (1215)	Mongol conquest of China (c. 1215-1368)	
	Hetum's alliance with Mongols (1247)	Ilkhanids (1256-1353)	Dominican order founded (1216)	Indian culture divided into Hindu and Muslim	
		Baghdad falls to Mongols End of Abbasid rule (1258)	St. Thomas Aquinas (1225-1274)	Kublai Khan (China) (1260-1294)	
	Levon II (1269-1289)		Louis IX (St. Louis) (1226-1270)	Marco Polo in China (c. 1275-1292)	
		Mongol defeat by Mamluks (1260)	Golden Horde (1226-1502)	Yuan Dynasty (China) (1279-1368)	
	Hetum II (1289-1293)	Peleologi emperors (1261-1453)	Edward I (1272-1307)	Japan halts Mongol invasion (1281)	
	Holy See moved to Sis (1292)	Last Crusader state falls to Muslims (1291)	Philip IV (The Fair) (1285-1314)		
			Mechanical clock (c. 1290)		
			Pope Boniface VIII (1294-1303)		

Table 9: 1100 A.D. to 1300 A.D.

X

East Meets West:

The Cilician Kingdom of Armenia (c. 1050-1375 A.D.)

The Cilician period, culminating in the establishment of the kingdom of Cilicia in 1199, represents a unique chapter in the history of the Armenian people. For the first and last time, Armenians living outside their homeland created an independent state. It is also the first time that Armenians were in a land with direct access to the sea and came into close contact with the emerging nations in Western Europe and the Roman Catholic Church.

Cilicia is a wide plain on the Mediterranean coast of Asia Minor. Surrounded by three mountain chains (the Taurus to the northwest, the Anti-Taurus to the northeast, and the Amanus to the east), Cilicia offered a secure enclave, for the narrow mountain passes, most famous of which was the Cilician Gates, were easily defended against invaders. The coastline and the navigable rivers, as well as a number of trade centers, made the region ideal for the Armenian merchants and farmers who were forced to leave Armenia in the eleventh century.

Armenians in Cilicia

Cilicia had been under Byzantine control since the mid-tenth century. After reconquering it from the Arabs, the Byzantines had expelled the Muslims from the fortresses and had brought in Christians, especially Armenians from Lesser Armenia, to repopulate the land. Following the

Byzantine and Turkish invasions of Armenia, more Armenians arrived in Cilicia, bringing their families and retinues. After the fall of the Bagratuni kingdom, the Byzantine empire assigned a number of Armenian military commanders to Cilicia. The Byzantines assigned them the duty of protecting this corridor to the heartland of Byzantium from Turkish and Arab attacks. Having lost their own fiefs, and being somewhat distant from the center of Byzantium and protected by mountains, a number of Armenian lords were able to achieve some level of independence.

Among these chieftains, two houses, the Rubenids and Hetumids, emerged as dominant forces and, by the end of the eleventh century, rivaled each other for the control of the plain. The Rubenids, who later claimed to be related to the Bagratunis, challenged Byzantine authority early on and controlled the mountainous region east of the Cilician Gates, with the fortress of Vahka as their headquarters. The Hetumids remained loyal vassals of Byzantium and maintained the fortresses of Lambron and Baberon as their power base. The Rubenids soon sought to extend their control southward to the lower plain with its trade routes and ports. This aggressive policy brought them into conflict with the Hetumids. It is at this time that an event occurred which helped Rubenid ambitions, the arrival of the West European forces of the First Crusade (1096-1099).

The Crusades and the Armenians

The crusades combined the political, religious, and economic ambitions of the West. In 1010, the Fatimid ruler of Egypt, al-Hakim, abrogated the spirit of the agreement reached in 807 A.D. by Harun al-Rashid and Charlemagne permitting pilgrimages to the Holy Places. Al-Hakim's persecution of Christians and the destruction of many churches, combined with armed conflicts among Muslim adventurers for the control of Syria and Jerusalem, made pilgrimages extremely difficult. The Seljuk conquest of Jerusalem in the late eleventh century actually brought some order, but the years of suffering had left a negative impression in Europe. The Byzantines, who were being attacked by the Seljuks, asked Europe for military aid in 1095, stating as one of their goals the restoration of Jerusalem to Christian control. Since in 1054 the Greek and Roman churches had split, a crusade into the Byzantine world would permit Rome to gain the upper hand in any future theological debate, and Byzantium's call was too tempting for Pope Urban II to resist. Moreover, the papacy had been involved in a bitter struggle with the German emperors over the leadership of Christian Europe. If the pope could gather a large army against the enemies of Christianity, his position would become paramount. In 1095 in Claremont, France, the pope called for a holy war. The result was the creation of a large army of lords and knights, clerics, adventurers, and the unemployed. Kings trying to establish order found the crusade an outlet to rid themselves of troublesome groups. Younger, landless, members of noble families who hoped to gain fiefs in the Middle East embraced the cause, while others sought financial rewards from supplies and commerce. For the pious, the assurance of a plenary papal indulgence was the primary motivation.

Neither the Muslims nor the Byzantines were prepared for such a group of devout Christians, able warriors, and plunderers. The Byzantine emperor immediately punished any looting and reminded the knights that any territory recovered was to revert to his control. The Muslims were distracted by a Shi'i-Sunni struggle between the Fatimids of Egypt and the forces of the caliph in Baghdad, and by the divisive ambitions of local emirs, who aspired to independent rule. Upon arrival in Cilicia, the corridor to Syria and Jerusalem, the crusaders sought out Armenians as guides, purveyors of supplies, and soldiers. By 1099 Jerusalem had fallen to the Christians, who massacred the Muslim inhabitants. The death of the papal legate left the region in the hands of the feudal barons, who soon divided it into the crusader or Latin states of Tripoli, Edessa, Antioch, and Jerusalem. Neither the Byzantines nor the Arabs were strong enough to resist the newcomers. The Rubenids allied themselves with the crusaders, who were called "Franks" by the natives, and established their own autonomous state in Cilicia. From the very beginning, the Armenian and crusader leaders had to deal with their own territorial ambitions. Edessa, which was controlled by an Armenian, for example, was taken over by Baldwin, who assumed the title of Count of Edessa. Other minor Armenian, Byzantine, and Arab chiefs soon lost their lands to the ambitious crusading lords of Antioch and Tripoli. The Rubenids and the Hetumids remained the only Armenian lords to control their own territories. Taking advantage of the situation, the Rubenids expanded at the expense of the Byzantines. Toros (1102-1129) captured the fortresses of Bardzberd and Anazarba from the Greeks and made it the center of Rubenid rule. His brother, Levon or Leo (1129-1137), expanded the Rubenid domains to the sea. A number of alliances with the Latin rulers, especially with Raymond of Antioch, kept the Rubenid position secure. In 1137, the Byzantine emperor, John Comnenus, after restoring Byzantine power in Serbia and Hungary, invaded Cilician Armenia on the way to Antioch, which was to have been turned over to Byzantium by the crusaders. The Hetumids cooperated with the emperor in capturing Rubenid fortresses and Antioch. Levon, his wife, and two sons named Ruben and Toros, were taken captive to Constantinople, while Count Raymond was left in Antioch as a vassal of Byzantium.

Levon, his wife, and Ruben, all died in captivity; but Toros managed to escape, returning to Cilicia where a few years later he managed to restore Rubenid power. His task was facilitated by the death of John Comnenus in 1143 and by the fall of Edessa to the Zangids, which prompted the unsuccessful Second Crusade in 1147-1149. The Armenians of Edessa escaped to Cilicia and Antioch, and Edessa was divided among the Byzantines and the Muslims. Around this time, the fortress of Hromkla (Rum Qalat), located on the Euphrates river, was granted to the Armenian catholicos by a noblewoman, and for the next one hundred years became the Holy See of the Armenians, despite the fact that for most of that time it was deep in Muslim-held territory.

Toros II (1144-1169) reclaimed his father's domain and, when the Byzantine-Antioch rapprochement suffered a setback, made an alliance with Reginald of Antioch. Emperor Manuel Comnenus, however, demanded the submission of Cilicia as a vassal state and invaded the region. Baldwin, now king of Jerusalem and related by marriage to the Byzantine emperor, mediated, and Toros kept his land as a nominal vassal. The rise of the Zangid state and its capture of Damascus under Nur al-Din, forced the Christians to abandon their differences and to seek common alliances. Toros managed to keep peace by remaining on good terms with both the Byzantines and the Muslims. He even tried an unsuccessful marriage alliance between the Rubenid and Hetumid families. His diplomacy and system of alliances created a strong Rubenid state recognized by the Byzantines and the Latin principalities.

Toros died in 1169 and his brother Mleh, who had converted to Islam, killed Toros' son, allied himself with Nur al-Din, and ruled Rubenid Cilicia. The death of the Zangi chief left Mleh powerless, and he was ousted in favor of Toros' nephew Ruben II (1175-1187). Ruben struggled with the Hetumids and the new count of Antioch, Bohemond. He was not an able ruler and abdicated in favor of his brother Levon who took over the family fortunes in 1187. Once again external events catapulted the Rubenids into a favorable position.

Saladin, a Turkicized Kurd, who had risen in the service of the Zangids, captured Cairo from the Fatimids in 1171, united it with Syria and established the Ayyubid dynasty. In 1187 he captured Jerusalem and although he spared Christian lives, his action launched the Third Crusade (1189-1192). This crusade, despite efforts of the pope, was primarily a lay and royal affair. The German ruler, Frederick Barbarossa, Richard I (the Lion-Hearted) of England, and Philip II Augustus of France led a great host of knights who managed to capture Acre but failed to retake Jerusalem. Frederick's formidable force disintegrated after he drowned in Cilicia. Saladin's favorable position and the rivalry between Richard and Philip, as well as their eventual departure, left only the narrow strip of coastal states of Antioch, Tripoli, and Tyre in Christian hands. Although the Third Crusade was a failure, one result of this episode was the capture of Cyprus by Richard and its sale to Guy de Lusignan, whose family would later become rulers of Cilician Armenia.

The Emergence of a New Armenian Kingdom

With the Latin states left vulnerable, Cilicia now assumed a new strategic importance, and European secular leaders requested its military and financial assistance to the crusading forces. Levon sought to use the situation to his advantage by seeking a royal crown. There is some evidence to indicate that a crown was promised to Levon by Frederick Barbarossa in exchange for his assistance during the Third Crusade. After some correspondence, Levon finally received a crown from Frederick's successor, the German Emperor Henry VI. He was crowned as King Levon I (Leo I) on 6 January 1199 in the Cathedral of Tarsus before the Rubenid, Hetumid, and crusader nobility. He was anointed by the catholicos and received the royal insignia from the papal and imperial legate, Conrad, archbishop of Mainz. A second crown arrived from the Byzantine emperor as a reminder that Byzantium still viewed Cilicia and its ruler as vassals.

Levon's coronation began a crisis which continued throughout the life of the kingdom: the question of religious unity with the Roman Catholic Church. Levon's crown came from the Holy Roman Emperor and was blessed by the pope, whom Western Europe viewed as the head of Christendom. There is no evidence of Levon agreeing to the supremacy of the Roman Church prior to his coronation. After the event, however, he asked the Armenian clergy to make a minor change in the Armenian liturgy and to concede a "special respect" to the pope as the successor of St. Peter. A move towards closer ties with Rome received the support of some of the clergy such as Bishop Nerses of Lambron, but after his death in 1199, the Armenian clergy rejected any compromise. The rift was to weaken the dynasty and was exploited by both the papacy and the crusaders.

Levon's elevation to the rank of king and its recognition by Europe literally put Cilicia on European maps, where it was referred to as "Little Armenia" or "Maritime Armenia." It also enabled Levon to gain the control of the Cilician plains and its ports. He broke the power of the Hetumids, established a new capital at Sis (see map 16), and managed to create a number of important marriage alliances with Cyprus, Antioch, and Byzantium. One such alliance, that with Antioch, proved problematic. Levon's niece, Alice, had married the son of Bohemond of Antioch, but was soon widowed and left with a son, Raymond-Ruben. Levon planned for an Armenian regency to take over Antioch and unite it with Cilicia after the death of Bohemond. The pope and the emperor initially supported Levon's plan, but the Italian merchants of Antioch and Bohemond's younger son, who ruled Tripoli, objected, and, after a three year war, ousted the young heir, Raymond-Ruben. Had Levon's plan succeeded, a powerful state would have emerged which might have altered the history of the region.

Such problems notwithstanding, Levon's rule created a kingdom

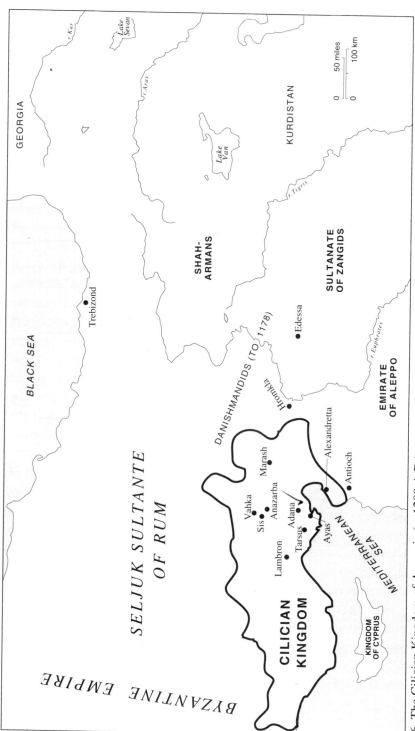

16. The Cilician Kingdom of Armenia (c. 1200 A.D.)

which was to last for almost two centuries. His relationship with the nobility was not based on the Armenian *nakharar* system, but on the Western feudal one of sovereign to vassal. Western feudal law was used to judge cases involving the court and nobility. In fact, the Assizes of Antioch, the main code of law used in the crusader states, has survived only in its Armenian translation. Nobles were knighted in the European tradition, and jousts and tournaments became popular. Latin and French terms of nobility and office replaced Armenian equivalents; for example, *paron* (baron) instead of *nakharar*, and *gonstapl* (constable) rather than *sparapet*. French and Latin became accepted languages at court. Even the Armenian alphabet was extended to accommodate the new sounds of "o" and "f," introduced by European languages. Western feudal dress became the norm, and French names became common among the courtiers and their wives. Finally, following the European custom of alliances, Armenian noblewomen married into major West European and Byzantine noble houses. Conversions to Catholicism or the Greek Orthodox faith became common among the nobles. These pro-Western tendencies were not imitated by the rest of Armenian society, however. Armenian merchants inter-married far less frequently, and the population at large, led by the Armenian Apostolic Church, was decidedly anti-Western. The catholicos with the aid of at least fourteen bishops, supervised the religious affairs of Cilicia from Hromkla. A number of Armenian monasteries were founded as well.

The most notable result of Levon's successful rule was the growth of commerce. Cilicia was a link for several trade routes from Central Asia and the Persian Gulf. Armenian merchants made contact with other traders and opened trading houses in China and Europe. European missionaries recorded that at this time Armenian churches were being built as far away as China. The port of Ayas on the Gulf of Alexandretta became the center of East-West commerce and is mentioned by Marco Polo as the starting point of his trip to China. Its bazaars sold dyes, silk, spices, cotton, wine, raisins, carpets, and pearls. Cilician goat-hair cloth, salt, iron, and timber were exported. Levon signed agreements with the Italian city states of Genoa, Venice, and Pisa, granting them tax exemptions in exchange for trade. The ports of Tarsus, Adana, and Mamistra were soon thriving cities full of foreign merchants, dominated by the Italians, who according to treaties, had their own trading houses, churches, and courts. Italian became the secondary language of Cilician commerce.

Levon died in 1219, leaving his only child, a daughter named Isabelle or Zabel, as his heir. At Levon's death, the situation in the Middle East was very different from the previous century. The Fourth Crusade (1202-1204), led by the Venetians, had not attacked the Muslims, but had captured and looted Constantinople, considerably weakening the Byzantine empire. Saladin's dynasty, the Ayyubid, was now a major force in Egypt, prompting the unsuccessful Fifth Crusade (1218-1221). The half-Armenian prince Raymond-Ruben, who had been driven out of Antioch, assumed the throne of Levon with the support of the pope, but was immediately ousted by the Armenian nobles, led by the Hetumids, who saw their chance of assuming control. Zabel was then married to Philip of Antioch with the understanding that he would adopt Armenian customs and become a member of the Armenian Church. Philip, however, disdained Armenian customs and spend most of his time in Antioch. The Armenian nobility decided to end the marriage; Philip was arrested and eventually poisoned. The Hetumid regent, Constantine, now arranged the marriage of Zabel to his own son, Hetum. Zabel, who seems to have been fond of Philip, fled the kingdom and even after her marriage to Hetum refused to live with her husband for some time. By 1226, however, the two were crowned at Sis and the Rubenid-Hetumid line was born.

Zabel and Hetum reigned from 1226 to 1252, Their joint reign was commemorated in coins bearing both their images, the second and last time the image of a woman was to appear on Armenian coinage. After Zabel's death, Hetum continued to rule until 1270, the longest rule of any Cilician king. Hetum's brother, Smbat, served as *sparapet* or constable and was an intimate and wise counselor to the king. Although the Ayyubids, and later the Mamluks, as well as the Seljuks, made periodic sorties against Cilicia, the era is known for its flowering of the arts. The most important political event of this period, however, was the arrival of the Mongols in the Middle East.

The Mongols and Cilician Armenia

The Mongols were united in 1206 by Genghis Khan, who managed in a short time to conquer half of Asia. Following his death in 1227, his son and grandson completed the conquest of China and Russia, and entered Eastern Europe, where they defeated Western armies in Poland, Hungary, and Germany, and reached the Adriatic Sea. Such an empire was obviously too large and diverse for one ruler, and the Mongols eventually divided their empire into four units. The first group ruled Mongolia, western Siberia, and Central Asia. The second, known as the Ilkhanids, controlled Persia, Armenia, Georgia, and the Middle East. The third, called the Golden Horde, occupied Russia, Ukraine, and parts of Poland, while the fourth moved to China and formed the Yuan dynasty under Kublai Khan, who acted as the head of the clan and did much to promote international trade (see map 17). The Ilkhanids, who were mostly shamanists, fought the Muslim Seljuks and Mamluks in the Middle East. The papacy, the crusaders, and the Armenians, therefore, made every effort to gain an alliance with the Mongols and at the same time convert them to Christianity.

Hetum was the first ruler who realized the importance of this new force in the area and sent his brother Smbat to the Mongol court at Karakorum. Smbat met Kublai's brother, Mongke Khan and, in 1247, made an alliance against the Muslims. On his return, Smbat passed through historic Armenia, the first time that any Cilician leader had seen his ancestral homeland. In 1254, Hetum visited Karakorum himself and renewed the alliance. The alliance helped Cilicia initially but, in 1260, the Mongols were defeated by the Mamluks and retreated to Persia. The Mamluks then attacked and devastated Cilicia. In 1269 Hetum abdicated in favor of his son Levon II (1269-1289), who was also forced to pay a large annual tribute to the Mamluks. The Mamluks continued their attacks during the reign of his son, Hetum II, and sacked Hromkla in 1292, prompting the Holy See to move to Sis. Hetum's sister married into the Lusignan family of Cyprus, and her children later inherited the Cilician Armenian throne. Hetum II, a devout Catholic, sought a closer union with Rome. His efforts did not materialize, and he abdicated first in favor of his brother and later of his nephew, Levon III. Although Cilicia enjoyed

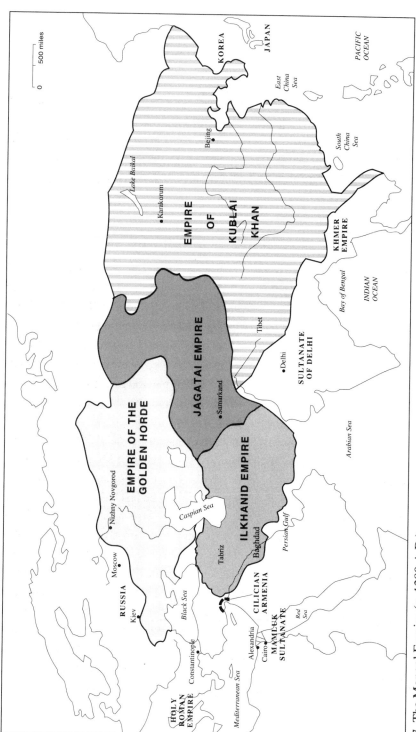

17. The Mongol Empire (c. 1280 A.D.)

a measure of economic prosperity under the Hetumids, the troubled reign of Hetum II caused a sense of political instability in the kingdom at a time when a strong effective leadership was badly needed to deal with the Muslim threat, for it was at this time that the Ilkhanid Mongols adopted Islam, the religion of the majority of their subject people. Hetum, now a Franciscan monk, together with Levon and forty Cilician nobles, made one more attempt at a Mongol alliance against the Mamluks. Upon their arrival at the Mongol headquarters in northern Syria, all forty-two were killed.

The Fall of Cilician Armenia

Yet another brother of Hetum, Oshin, assumed the throne and convened the Church councils at Sis in 1307 and Adana in 1316 where a number of Armenian clergy and nobles, hoping to receive military aid from Europe, agreed to conform to Roman liturgical practices and recognize the pope. The Armenian population rose against this decision, and Oshin was poisoned in 1320. His son Levon IV, who was even more strongly pro-Western, was also killed in 1341. There were now no direct descendants of the Rubenid-Hetumid line left, and the throne passed to the Lusignans of Cyprus.

A number of Lusignans, all named Constantine, ruled for brief periods and made concessions to the Mamluks in exchange for short periods of peace. Most were murdered by rivals, court intrigue, or by Armenian leaders suspicious of non-Armenian rulers. The last Cilician king, Levon V, was crowned at Sis in 1374, but one year later was captured with his family by the Mamluks, who took him to Cairo from where he was ransomed by his European relatives. Levon attempted to revive the crusader spirit in Europe, but died in France in 1393 and was buried with the kings of France in the church of St. Denis, in Paris. Ironically Levon's title of king of Armenia passed to John I of Cyprus, whose descendants then passed it on to the House of Savoy; they used the title as late as the nineteenth century. The Cilician Armenian nobility left for Byzantium, Armenia, and Georgia, while Armenian merchants immigrated to France, Holland, Italy, and Poland. A century later Cilicia became part of the Ottoman empire.

The Armenian Community of Jerusalem

One of the consequences of the rise of the Cilician kingdom was a new prominence for the Armenian secular and religious community of Jerusalem. An Armenian presence in that city can be traced back as far as the first centuries of the Christian era. By the seventh century numerous Armenian monasteries had been built there. After the break with the Greek Orthodox Church, Armenians were subject to discrimination by the city's Byzantine rulers. Following the Arab conquest in 638 A.D., control over the Christian holy places of Jerusalem became the avenue to and symbol of power for the city's Armenian and Greek communities. Although the Armenians in Jerusalem numbered fewer than the Greeks, they enjoyed better relations with the Arabs, who saw the Byzantines as their common enemy. The Armenian Church was, therefore, initially granted custodianship of a number of important Christian shrines, although disagreements between the Greek Orthodox and Armenian Churches over their control continued through the years. The arrival of the crusaders improved the Armenians' position considerably and enabled them to acquire a site from the Georgian Church over which they built the cathedral and monastery of St. James and founded the monastic order of the Brotherhood of St. James. St. James became the heart of Jerusalem's Armenian community, providing accommodations for pilgrims and visiting merchants. At the beginning of the fourteenth century, the St. James Brotherhood refused to accept the Latinophile policies of the catholicosate of Cilicia and proclaimed its head the Armenian patriarch of Jerusalem, and the guardian of the Armenian-controlled holy places. The Armenians retained their favored status and were exempted from the *jizya* after the Muslims retook Jerusalem under Saladin. During the Mamluk period the Armenians managed to forestall attempts by the Georgian Orthodox Church to take over St. James, but were forced to share custodianship of parts of the Holy Sepulchre with the Georgian and Greek Churches.

Arts and Culture

Cilicia was home to a variety of peoples, all of whom contributed to the richness of Cilician culture. Greeks, Syrian Jacobites, Arabs, and Jews lived in the region, each supporting their own religious institutions. Italian merchants and European knights made their home in or frequented the ports of Cilicia. The French language and customs had spread among the Armenian nobility and Italian was spoken by all merchants. European works, including histories, written originally in Latin, found their way into Armenian translations. The Assizes of Antioch, the code of law used in the Crusader states, has survived only in its Armenian translation. A number of original works are significant as well. The *Chronicle* of Constable Smbat, the brother of Hetum I, is the most valuable account of the Cilician kingdom. His revision of the Armenian law code of Mkhitar Gosh, as well as his account of his trip to the court of the Mongols, are important as well. Hetum, the Historian, a nephew of Hetum I, offers another valuable account. Known as the *Little Chronicle* and written in 1307, it contains an historical and geographical survey of Asia, followed by a history of the Mongols, focusing in particular on the conflicts between the Ilkhans and the Mamluks, and concluding with a plan for a new crusade. A noteworthy work on the earlier history of Cilicia is the *Chronicle* of Matthew of Edessa (Matevos Urhaetsi). Catholicos Nerses, known as *Shnorhali* (the Gracious), left his *Lamentations on the Fall of Edessa*, as well as many *sharakans* or hymns used in the Armenian mass. Poetry, including poems on love and other secular themes, appeared in the last two centuries of Cilician Armenia. Those of John of Erzinga (Hovhannes Erzingatsi) were written in the early Armenian vernacular, sometimes referred to as Middle Armenian.

What has survived of Cilician architecture resembles crusader castles and fortresses and copies Byzantine and Western edifices of the period. Although no significant sculpture has survived from Cilicia, reliquary and silver bible bindings from the thirteenth century display the craftsmanship of Cilicia's silversmiths. The glory of the period, however, is undoubtedly its illuminated manuscripts from the twelfth and thirteenth centuries. Humans, animals, flowers, and geometric designs are depicted in rich colors and glittering gold. The most renowned are those of Toros Roslin, who used contemporary costumes and naturalism in biblical themes and combined both Asian and European motifs.

There are a number of reasons for the rise and fall of the Armenian kingdom of Cilicia. The geographical position of Cilicia, the arrival of Armenian feudal families, and the temporary weakness of Byzantium permitted the rise of the Rubenids and Hetumids. The coming of the crusades gave the Armenians sufficient political, economic, and strategic importance to form first, a principality and later, a kingdom. The failure of successive crusades, division among the Christian forces and the refusal of the Armenian Church to accept Roman suzerainty, the rise of the Ayyubid and Mamluk states, the fall of the last crusader bastion in 1291, as well as the conversion of the Ilkhanid Mongols to Islam, all contributed to the fall of the Armenian kingdom. By the fourteenth century, Europe had become involved in its own state-building. The expulsion of the Muslims out of much of Spain spelled the end of the crusading spirit, and Europe largely abandoned its interests in the Christians living in Asia. This was to have major repercussions for the West, for the Ottoman Turks would soon destroy Byzantium and enter Eastern Europe, where they would remain for some four centuries.

C.E.	(Historic and Cilicia) ARMENIA	ISLAMIC MIDDLE EAST & BYZANTIUM	EUROPE	INDIA, CHINA & JAPAN	SUB-SAHARAN AFRICA & THE AMERICAS
1300	Council of Sis (1307) Oshin (1307-1320) Council of Adana (1316) Guy de Lusignan (1342-1344) Levon V (1374-1375) Fall of Cilician Armenian Kingdom (1375) Timur's invasions of Armenia (1386-1403)	Ottoman conquests in Anatolia (c. 1300-1395) Murad I (1362-1389) Persian poet Hafiz (d. 1389) Bayazid I (1389-1402)	Petrarch (1304-1374) Avignon papacy (1305-1378) Dante's Divine Comedy (c. 1310) Hundred Years' War (1337-1453) Black Death (1347-1350) Italian Renaissance (c. 1350-1550) Hanseatic League (c. 1350-1450) Boccaccio's Decameron (c.1350) Great Schism (1378-1417) Medici Bank (1397-1494) Chaucer's Canterbury Tales (c. 1390)	Rise of Daimyo in Japan (c. 1300-1500) Ashikage Shogunate in Japan (1336-1573) Ming Dynasty in China (1368-1644) Timur sacks Delhi (1398)	Stone complexes in Zimbabwe (c. 1300) Aztecs arrive in Mexico (c. 1325) University of Timbuktu (c. 1330) Kong Kingdom in Africa (c. 1350)
1400	Holy See returns to Etchmiadzin (1441) Qara-Qoyunlu in Armenia (c. 1380-1468) Aq-Qoyunlu in Armenia (c. 1468-1500)	Timur's invasions of Anatolia (1400-1402) Ibn-Khaldun (d. 1406) Mehmet II (1451-1481) Ottomans capture Constantinople, end of Byzantine rule (1453) Ottoman Empire (1453-1918)	Council of Constance (1414-1417) Hussite revolt (1420-1434) Joan of Arc (active 1429-1431) Council of Basel (1431-1449) Botticelli (1444-1510) Printing press (c. 1450) Leonardo da Vinci (1452-1519) War of the Roses (1455-1485) Ivan III of Russia (1462-1505) Erasmus (c. 1467-1536) Machiavelli (1469-1527) Union of Ferdinand and Isabella (1469) Dürer (1471-1528) Raphael (1483-1520) Martin Luther (1483-1546) Tudor Dynasty in England (1485-1603) Michelangelo (1485-1564) Loyola (1491-1556) Fall of Granada, last Muslim state in Spain (1492)	Muslims establish commercial center at Malacca (c. 1400) Vasco da Gama reaches India (1498) Sikh religious sect founded (1498)	Height of Inca power in Peru (1438-1532) Height of Aztec power in Mexico (c. 1440) Portugese arrive in Benin (c. 1440) Height of Songhai Empire in Africa (1468-1590) Diaz rounds the Cape of Good Hope (1488) Columbus discovers New World (1492)

Table 10: 1300 A.D. to 1500 A.D.

XI

From Majority To Minority:

Armenia Under Turkish, Mongol, and Turkmen Domination (c. 1050-1500)

During the nearly five hundred years between the arrival of the Turks in Armenia and the establishment of the Safavi dynasty in Persia, Europe made the transition from the Middle Ages to the Modern Period. In the Middle East, 'Abbasid rule continued for another two centuries. The caliphate was in decline, and various Turkish, Kurdish, and Persian military leaders had established their own dynasties. The arrival of the Seljuk Turks resulted in the emergence of a powerful Islamic state. By the second half of the thirteenth century, the entire situation had changed when the Mongols conquered Baghdad, ending the 'Abbasid caliphate. The Turks, under the leadership of the Ottomans, revived in Anatolia and eventually took Constantinople toppling the Byzantine empire.

The same period in Western Europe witnessed changes which, in the modern or post-1500 period, enabled it to assume the military and economic leadership of the world. The rise of trade, cities, and the middle class, prepared the ground for representative government. The captivity of the Papacy in Avignon, the Hundred Years War, the Black Death, and the War of the Roses weakened the Roman Catholic Church and facilitated the rise of strong monarchies. The Renaissance enabled Europe to discover its Greco-Roman traditions, fostered a spirit of individualism, and set the stage for scientific advances and artistic expression. In the meantime, the same centuries saw the gradual reconquest of Spain, culminating in the fall of Granada in 1492. Ironically, the Ottomans were reviving the Muslim presence in Europe by penetrating Eastern and Central Europe. The first Russian state was crushed by the Mongols, who ruled there for three centuries and who passed on some of their socio-political institutions to the future Russian state. Both the Ottoman conquests and the Ming dynasty's isolationist policy in China, closed the land trade routes with Asia and pushed Europe into the Age of Exploration. With considerable help from Chinese technology, Columbus and Vasco de Gama found both the Americas and the sea route to India and China.

In Africa, Egypt championed the cause of Islam against the Mongols and the Crusaders. Islam managed to penetrate sub-Saharan regions and became the major religion of North and Central Africa. The kingdoms and states of Mali, Benin, Yoruba, and Songhai flourished until the European penetration, which began when the west coast of Africa was explored by the Portuguese at the end of this period.

India, which had experienced the Arab invasions of Sind in the early seventh century, was invaded by new Muslim armies, who conquered northern India, established the Sultanate of Delhi, ended the influence of Buddhism, and divided India into Muslim and Hindu cultures. In southeast Asia, the Khmer empire reached its peak with the construction of Angkor Wat, and Vietnam gained its independence from China.

In China itself, the Sung dynasty lost control of the north to the Chin dynasty, and both were later conquered by the Mongols, who established the Yuan dynasty. Kublai Khan adopted Chinese culture, moved his capital to Beijing, and was visited by Marco Polo. The new empire established the *pax Mongolica*, which facilitated East-West trade and the transfer of technology to Western Europe. A century later, the Mongols were driven out of China by the Ming Dynasty, which at first encouraged trade and explorations, but later closed China to all foreigners. In Japan, two successive *shogunates* ruled successfully, keeping Japan isolated and defending it against Mongol invasions. Finally, in the Americas, the Inca empire in Peru and the Aztecs in Mexico had blossomed into major organized states.

In contrast, historic Armenia was entering the nadir of its history. The last Armenian dynasty had fallen, and a great number of nobles, soldiers, and artisans had left for Constantinople, Cilicia, and eastern Europe.

Furthermore, the next four centuries witnessed the arrival of thousands of nomadic invaders which would had a major effect on the history of Armenia and the Armenians.

Turks in Armenia

Turkic bands from Central Asia, particularly the Oghuz tribe, had been slowly raiding and settling parts of Azerbaijan, the northern Caucasus, southern Russia, and even northern Asia Minor since the tenth century. The Byzantine policy of weakening Armenia by removing its military forces had left the region undefended and had invited marauding Turkish groups to attack southern Armenia. Until the arrival of the Seljuks in the mid-eleventh century, there was no organized Turkish plan to conquer Armenia. Between 1040 and 1045, an Oghuz chief, Toghrul of the Seljuk family, conquered most of Persia and founded an empire. The Seljuks soon faced a problem which confronted all nomadic conquerors after they had settled down in their new territories, namely, how to deal with those in their tribes who wanted to continue to raid and plunder. The Seljuks, fearing the destruction of their new empire, directed the energies of their undisciplined elements to undefended Armenia in the hope of gaining new territory. Thus, for the next two decades Armenia was periodically attacked.

The Armenians and Byzantines fought the invaders, but unfortunately, not together. The Byzantines did not realize the gravity of the situation but, rather, tried to abolish any form of Armenian autonomy and bring the Armenian Church under the control of Constantinople. At times, Byzantine actions even spurred some Armenians to cooperate with the Turks against the Byzantines. In 1071 the Seljuk army under the command of Alp Arslan, defeated and captured the Byzantine emperor Romanus IV Diogenes. The Byzantines, who had destroyed the Bagratuni kingdom a few years before, now lost it to the Turks. Many cities were looted, churches destroyed, trade disrupted, and the population forcibly converted or enslaved. A number of dynasties such as the Danishmendids, Qaramanids, Shah-Armans, and the Seljuks of Rum emerged in Anatolia. The nakharars of Artsakh (Karabagh), Siunik (Zangezur), Gugark (Lori), Sasun, and other mountainous regions, however, maintained viable military forces and remained autonomous. A number of *nakharars* left with their families and retinue and established new centers of power in Georgia and Cilicia. Not all Armenian conversions to Islam were forced; some Armenian artisans and military men converted voluntarily for economic reasons. Intermarriage between the Turkish and Armenian upper classes also contributed to such conversions. In fact, a number of independent emirates in eastern Anatolia were of Armenian descent. The bulk of the Armenian population, the peasantry, however, remained Christian.

The prestige of the Seljuks reached new heights when they captured Jerusalem and received the title of *sultan* from the caliph. They soon employed Persian viziers, adopted Persian titles, and began to view themselves as monarchs of a centralized state. Armenians and settled Muslims were protected, and trade somewhat revived. By the mid-twelfth century, when the Persian Seljuks were overthrown by other Turkic nomads, the situation had changed considerably in favor of the Christians. The crusades had established a strong Christian presence in the Middle East, Georgia was rising as a power in Transcaucasia, the Armenians of Cilicia were creating a viable state, and Byzantium revived under the Comneni emperors. The Turkic groups had also become fragmented into small states scattered in Asia Minor and Transcaucasia.

The period between the decline of the Seljuks and the arrival of the Mongols was a time of revival for the Armenians. The main impetus was the emergence of Georgia and its Bagratuni dynasty, who were of Armenian descent, as the pre-eminent power in Transcaucasia and eastern Anatolia. The Georgians, under David the Builder (1089-1125), recruited Armenian *nakharars* from the Artsruni, Pahlavuni, Zakarian, Orbelian, and Proshian families, as well as the dispossessed *azats*, who joined the Georgian army to expel the Turkic nomads from Armenia. David's successors continued this policy and eventually resettled much of Armenia with their Armenian volunteers. Under Queen Tamar (1184-1213), the Zakarians, who commanded the Armeno-Georgian forces, succeeded in conquering much of Greater Armenia. The Zakarians ruled Armenia from Ani and Dvin as vassals of the Georgian monarchs (see map 18). Most of the other *nakharars* submitted to Zakarid leadership. The coronation of Leo and the official recognition of the Cilician Armenian Kingdom by Europe in 1199, opened the trade routes from Europe to

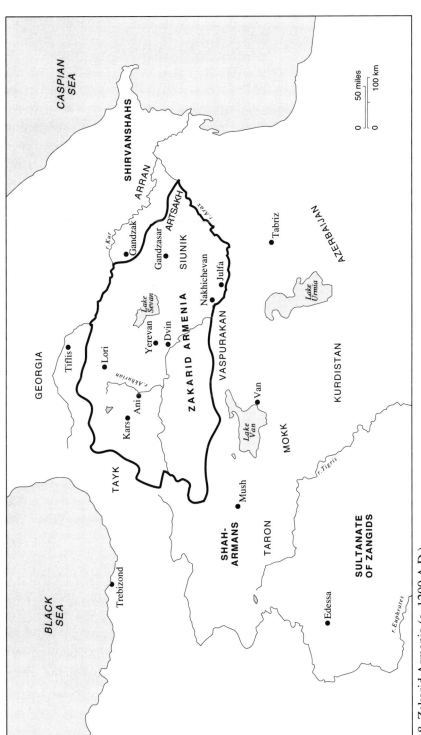

18. Zakarid Armenia (c. 1200 A.D.)

Asia via Armenia and Georgia and brought new wealth to the region. The Zakarians inter-married into a number of *nakharar* families and, like the Georgians kings, established courts with their own hierarchy. For the first time, new Armenian *nakharars* had emerged, men who were not part of the old feudal houses, but who had risen through military or commercial achievements. They purchased or were assigned lands and became benefactors of cultural and religious institutions. With the Holy See in Cilicia, new Church leaders emerged in historic Armenia. Artisans lived in the cities, where they received some rights and established guilds. The peasants, as in the past, remained attached to the soil and paid most of the taxes. Unfortunately for Armenia and Georgia, these prosperous days were short-lived. As noted, a new force made its appearance in world history, a force which not only ended the Armeno-Georgian interlude, but drastically altered the history of Russia and the Middle East: the Mongols.

Mongols in Armenia

A decade prior to the major Mongol invasion of Transcaucasia, a small Mongol force had defeated the Armeno-Georgian army and had looted the region. In their eastward march, the Mongols had pushed Turkic tribes westward. Some of the latter then entered Armenia and used it as a base from which to resist the Mongols. Although the Armenians, Georgians, and even Muslims succeeded in ousting the invaders, the loss of life and destruction of property and crops was severe. It was at this juncture that the main Mongol armies appeared in 1236. The Mongols swiftly conquered the cities; those which resisted were cruelly punished, while those submitting were rewarded. News of this spread quickly and resulted in the submission of all of historic Armenia and parts of Georgia by 1245. The Muslim rulers of western Armenia were crushed as well.

During the period of consolidation, the shamanistic Mongols did not impose their taxes or administrative structure until the mid-thirteenth century, when they conducted a census and heavily taxed all the inhabitants, Muslims and Christians. A number of uprisings were put down severely. Armenian and Georgian military leaders had to serve in the Mongol army, where many of them perished in battle. The Mongols also managed to attract a number of *nakharars* to enter their service. The Orbelians of Siunik and Hasan-Jalalians of Artsakh were the most notable of these. The Mongols played the *nakharars* against each other, and occasionally used Muslims against Christians or vice-versa, to achieve their goals. In 1258 the Ilkhanid Mongols under the leadership of Hulagu, sacked Baghdad and killed many Muslims. Ironically, this action provoked the anger of another Mongol group, the Golden Horde, who had conquered Russia and who had converted to Islam. Following the defeat of the Ilkhanid Mongols by the Mamluks in Syria in 1260, the two Mongol groups clashed in the Caucasus.

The Armenian Church was generally spared the havoc of this period. A number of Mongol leaders had become Nestorian Christians and had thus a special sympathy for the Armenians, whom they probably viewed as fellow Monophysites. Armenian monasteries and clergy were periodically exempted from taxes. The privileges granted by the Mongols were later cited by the Armenian Church leaders to help gain considerable concessions from the Mongol and Turkmen khans who ruled the land during the fourteenth and fifteenth centuries. Armenian merchants were also treated well by the Mongols. The Chinese Mongols encouraged trade, and Italian merchants from Venice and Genoa used Cilician or Black Sea ports to conduct a significant trade with China. Caravans were guarded and the Mongols assured safe passage through Central Asia. Silk, gems, and spices were the main exports. Armenian merchants opened trading branches in Beijing, Tabriz, Sultanieh, Bukhara, Trebizond, as well in a number of cities in Russia and Italy.

By 1300 the Ilkhanids had accepted Islam, and Armenians were once again treated as infidels. Taxes were increased, Armenians had to wear special badges to identify them as Christians, and large fertile areas were reserved for nomadic tribes, destroying the agricultural economy and forcing starvation and poverty. The collapse of the Ilkhanids in the mid-fourteenth century only worsened the situation. Various tribal groups attacked eastern Armenia, while the Ottomans Turks began their subjugation of western Armenia.

Timur and Turko-Tatars in Armenia

The final blow was left to the last great invader from Central Asia, Lame Timur or, as he is known in the West, Tamerlane. Between 1386 and 1403 Timur, a Turkicized Mongol, and his Turko-Tatar hordes invaded Armenia, devastating cities, destroying crops, killing tens of thousands and enslaving even more. He even fought the Turkmen tribes who had settled in the region, defeated the Golden Horde and delivered a devastating blow to the Ottomans. The destruction was more severe than anything else before and reduced Armenia to rubble. Many cities and villages simply disappeared. Trade ceased completely, and Armenian churchmen, merchants, and *nakharars* were put to death. Only the mountainous regions of Artsakh, Gugark, Siunik, Sasun, and Mush survived the pillage, some of their inhabitants later turning to banditry in order to survive. Timur took many Armenian artisans to Samarkand where they helped to build his great capital city. Although he conquered Delhi, his aim was to loot and not to stay. After Timur's death, his family members ruled in the eastern Caucasus and Central Asia, but a later Timurid, Babur, conquered Delhi in 1526 and began the great Mughal dynasty which ruled until 1858. Ironically, as will be noted in volume II, Armenian merchants played a vital role in Indian trade during the Mughal period.

The vacuum left by the death of Timur was filled by the Ottomans, Timurids, Shirvanshahs, Aq-Qoyunlu, Qara-Qoyunlu, and the few remaining Georgian princes. The Ottomans concentrated their efforts on what was left of the Byzantine empire. In 1453 Mehmet the Conqueror took Constantinople, and the Ottomans began their rise, culminating in the capture or control of the entire Middle East, most of north Africa and much of Eastern Europe. Only Persia and the eastern parts of Armenia and Georgia eluded them. The Shirvanshahs controlled part of present-day Azerbaijan, while the Timurids, their nominal suzerains, had their base in eastern Persia. Historic Armenia fell into the realm of two Turkmen tribes, Qara-Qoyunlu and Aq-Qoyunlu, which had been in the region prior to Timur. The Qara-Qoyunlu, or Black Sheep, who had Shi'i sympathies, controlled the region east of Lake Van until 1468. The Timurids and the Qara-Qoyunlu fought each other and continued to wreak havoc on Armenia and Georgia. Two Qara-Qoyunlu rulers, Iskandar (1420-1438) and Jihan Shah (1438-1468), had friendly relations with the Armenian Church and a number of *nakharars*, which resulted in the return of the Holy See to Etchmidzin in 1441. The move, which eventually was to be challenged by the Cilician religious hierarchy, made Edjmiadsin, and later, the Armenian Patriarchate in Constantinople, the official political and cultural centers of the Armenian people. The Aq-Qoyunlu, or White Sheep, controlled all the Armenian lands west of Lake Van to the Euphrates River. They conquered the Qara-Qoyunlu in 1468 and ruled over all of Armenia, Azerbaijan, most of Georgia, and a major part of Persia until the end of the fifteenth century, when they were replaced by the Safavids. The Aq-Qoyunlu under Uzun Hasan (1453-1478) forced the Armenians to wear clothing which distinguished them as Christians and taxed them heavily. Worse conditions arose under Ya'qub (1478-1490), who levied large new taxes. Most of the last remaining *nakharars* had their lands confiscated or, to save their holdings, donated it to the Church as *waqf* or endowment. Some became churchmen, while others accumulated whatever capital they could muster and went into trade. A handful of minor nobles or scions of larger houses, such as the princes of Khachen, kept their holdings in the highlands of Karabagh and Zangezur. A number of Kurdish tribes from Persia and Syria joined earlier arrivals in Armenia. The economic hardships notwithstanding, the Aq-Qoyunlu restored order, and peace returned to Armenia, enabling the population to recover somewhat before the next round of wars between the Ottomans and the Safavids.

At the close of the Middle Ages, Armenian political presence had thus gradually waned in Armenia. The demographic changes, which had begun in the eleventh century and which would continue uninterrupted to the dawn of the seventeenth century, would finally result in the Armenians being reduced to a minority in their own homeland.

Literature, Learning, and Art

Despite four hundred years of invasions and devastation, Armenians still managed to produce historical and literary works. The major historians of the thirteenth century were Kirakos Gandzaketsi and Vardan

Areveltsi. Gandzaketsi was captured by the Mongols, and learned their language, and his history is a primary source for the Mongol and Zakarid period in Armenia. Arevelsti visited the Mongol court in Central Asia and befriended Hulagu in Persia. Another important historian of this period is Stepanos Orbelian, a bishop and a member of the Siuni family who also visited the Mongol court and who wrote *The History of the Family and the Province of Siunik*. Grigor Akants wrote an interesting history of the Mongols, entitled the *History of the Nation of the Archers*. Finally, Tovma Metsobetsi wrote the *History of Tamerlane and His Successors*, which details the terrible devastation of Armenia by the Turkmen. In the literary arena, Frik, a layman poet, described in the vernacular the sufferings of the people during the Mongol invasions.

One result of the numerous invasions and occupations of Armenia was the Armenians being forced to learn Persian, Turkish, Mongol, Georgian, and Uigur and often acted as interpreters in trade and at court. European travelers mention Armenian translators and middle men in Central Asia, India, and at the various Mongol courts. Monasteries, as before, served as centers of learning. Tatev and Gladzor, both in Siunik, can be viewed as proto-universities where the arts and sciences, as well as religious studies were taught. These centers were especially active against the inroads of Catholic missionaries. In the fourteenth century, the Dominicans had succeeded in converting a number of Armenian laymen and clergy in Nakhichevan and had founded the *Fratres Unitores* (in Armenian, *unitork*), an Armenian Catholic branch of the Dominican order. The Armenian theologians from Gladzor played an important part in resisting and limiting these Latin influences in Armenia.

These chaotic times did not hinder trade or the construction of churches. One of the trade routes passed through Georgia and northern Armenia to Trebizond, from where it continued to Venice and Genoa. Armenian merchants were active in this trade and accumulated considerable wealth, part of which found its way into donations to monasteries and the construction of churches. The churches of Noravank, Khorakert, Areni, Eghvard and a number of later churches in Ani are of this period. A number of monasteries were completed as well: Sanahin, Hovhnannavank, Harijavank, Haghardsin, Spitakavor, Tegher, Kecharis, Goshavank, and Geghard. Finally, the Holy See of Gandzasar in Artsakh (Karabagh)

was constructed in this period. Relief sculpture in stucco or stone geometric designs, interlacing real and imaginary animals, as had appeared on palaces and churches during the Bagratuni period, now emerged in a more mature form. Silver bindings and reliquaries, especially those commissioned by the Proshian family, evidence the art of silversmiths. The art of making *khachkars*, as noted earlier, reached its peak in this period. Illuminated manuscripts were influenced in their ornamental composition by Cilician works; the Gospel of Haghpat and the Gospel of Gladzor are fine examples from this period.

Conclusion

For over two thousand years Armenia's geographical position and the adaptable nature of its people enabled it to maintain a unique place in the ancient, classical, and medieval periods. Armenia supported a number of dynasties, developed its own art and architecture, language and literature, and was the first state to adopt Christianity as its official religion, a decision which affected the rest of its history. In a small way, Armenia contributed to the Western European Renaissance through the preservation of a number of classical works and in serving as a conduit of goods and ideas from the East to the West. Armenian contacts with China may have even aided the transference of some of the technology which contributed to the discovery of the new world.

At the dawn of the modern period, as the West began to explore a new world and adopt new ideas, the East entered a gradual period of hibernation and decline. Armenia, which in the past had been at the forefront of cultural exchange, was cut off from the West by the Ottomans. Four centuries of nomadic invasions had turned most of Armenia into a leaderless and bleak landscape, its people a minority in their own homeland. Now, but a small Christian enclave in a sea of Muslims and nomads, Armenia and its inhabitants fell into a stagnation which lasted until the nineteenth century.

With much of Armenia's talent voluntarily or forcibly migrating, its diaspora now became a major force. It was in the major cities of Europe and Asia, that the Armenians maintained much of their national spirit, and it was in the diaspora that the revival of Armenian culture and the next, crucial, chapters of Armenian history would be played out.

1. Uratian Helmets

2. Bronze Head of
Hellenistic Diety

3. Silver Coin of Tigran II

4. Temple of Garni

5. Cathedral of Etchmiadzin

Ա ա	a		Ծ ծ	ds		Ջ ջ	dj
Բ բ	b		Կ կ	k		Ռ ռ	r
Գ գ	g		Հ հ	h		Ս ս	s
Դ դ	d		Ձ ձ	dz		Վ վ	v
Ե ե	e		Ղ ղ	gh		Տ տ	t
Զ զ	z		Ճ ճ	j		Ր ր	ŕ
Է է	e		Մ մ	m		Ց g	ts
Ը ը	e		Յ յ	h, y or –		Ւ ւ	v
Թ թ	t		Ն ն	n		Փ փ	p
Ժ ժ	zh		Շ շ	sh		Ք ք	k
Ի ի	i		Ո ո	vo or o		Օ օ	o
Լ լ	l		Չ չ	ch		Ֆ ֆ	f
Խ խ	kh		Պ պ	p			

6. The Armenian Alphabet

7. Church of St. Hripsimé

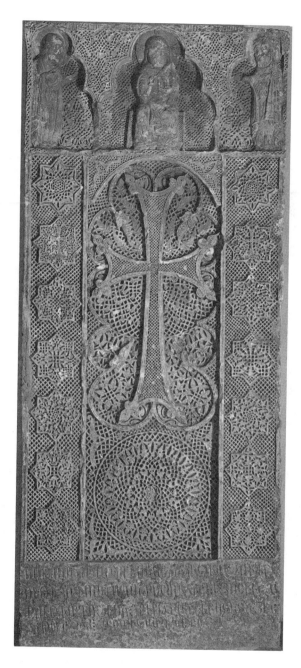

8. Khachkar (14th Century)

9. Cathedral of Ani

10. Fortress of Vahka

11. Last Judgment by Toros Roslin

12. Monastery of Geghard

13. David & Goliath, Church of Holy Cross, Aghtamar

Selected Bibliographical Guide

General:

The Cambridge History of Iran, Vols. I-V. Cambridge, 1968-1985; *The Cambridge Ancient History*, (12 vols.). Cambridge, 1971-1992; *The Cambridge Medieval History*, (9 vols.). Cambridge, 1911-1967; C. E. Bosworth, *The Islamic Dynasties*. Edinburgh, 1967; Academy of Sciences of Armenia, *The History of the Armenian People*, Vols. I-IV (in Armenian). Yerevan, 1971-1984; G. Dédéyan, ed., *Histoire des Arméniens*. Toulouse, 1982; T. Kh. Hakobian, *Armenia's Historical Geography* (in Armenian). Yerevan, 1968; Leo, *History of Armenia*, Vols I-II (in Armenian). Yerevan, 1966-1967; H. Manandian, *A Critical Study of the History of the Armenian People*, 3 vols in 4 parts (in Armenian). Yerevan, 1946-1952; C. Toumanoff, *Studies in Christian Caucasian History*. Georgetown, 1963.

Armenian historians (English translations):

Agathangelos, *History of the Armenians* (R. W. Thomson). Albany, 1976; P'awstos Buzand, *The Epic Histories* (N. G. Garsoian). Harvard, 1989; P'awstos Buzandac'i, *History of the Armenians* (R. G. Bedrosian). New York, 1985; Koriun, *Life of Mashtots* (B. Norehad). New York, 1964; Moses Khorenatsi, *History of the Armenians* (R. W. Thomson). Cambridge, Mass., 1978; Egishe Vardapet, *History of Vardan and the Armenian War* (R. W. Thomson). Cambridge, Mass., 1982; Tovma Artsruni, *History of the House of the Artsrunik'* (R. W. Thomson).

Detroit, 1985; Hovhannes Draskhanakertetsi, *History of Armenia* (K. H. Maksoudian). Atlanta, 1987; Ghazar P'arbec'i, *History of the Armenians* (R. G. Bedrosian). New York, 1985; Sebeos, *History* (R. G. Bedrosian). New York, 1985; John Mamikonean, *History of Taron* (R. G. Bedrosian). New York, 1985; Aristakes Lastivertc'i, *History* (R. G. Bedrosian). New York, 1985; Kirakos Gandzakets'i, *History of the Armenians* (R. G. Bedrosian). New York, 1986; T'ovma Metsobets'i, *History of Tamerlane and his Successors* (R. G. Bedrosian). New York, 1987; *The Fables of Mkhitar Gosh* (R. G. Bedrosian). New York, 1987; *The Georgian Chronicle* (R. G. Bedrosian). New York, 1991; and the translation of the Armenian epic *Daredevils of Sassoun* (L. Surmelian). New York, 1964, *David of Sassoun* (A. K. Shalian). Athens, Ohio, 1964.

On the pre-Urartuan period and the Urartian kingdom see:
C. Burney and D. M. Lang, *The Peoples of the Hills: Ancient Ararat and the Caucasus*. New York, 1972; B. B. Piotrovskii, *Urartu: The Kingdom of Van and its Art*. New York, 1967; and his *The Ancient Civilization of Urartu: An Archeological Adventure*. New York, 1969; G. Azarpay, *Urartian Art and Artifacts: A Chronological Study*. Berkeley, 1968; T. V. Gamkrelidze and V. V. Ivanov, *Indo-European and Indo-Europeans: A Reconstruction and Historical Typological Analysis of a Protolanguage and Proto-Culture*. 2 vols. (in Russian) Tbilisi, 1984; C. Renfrew, *Archeology and Language: The Puzzle of Indo-European Origins*. Cambridge, 1988.

On the Median, Achaemenid, Yervanduni, Seleucid, Artashesian, Parthian, Arshakuni, and Sasanid periods, see:
P. Z. Bedoukian, *Coinage of the Artaxiads of Armenia*. London, 1978; N. C. Debevoise, *A Political History of Parthia*. Chicago, 1938; Herodotus, *The History* (trans. G. Rawlinson). New York, 1943; R. N. Frye, *The Heritage of Persia*. London, 1962; N. Garsoian, "Byzantium and the Sasanians" in *Cambridge History of Iran* (Vol. 3, pt. 1); D. M. Lang, "Iran, Armenia and Georgia," in *Cambridge History of Iran* (vol. 3 pt 1); H. Manandian, *Tigrane II et Rome* (Lisbon, 1963); A. T. Olmstead, *History of the Persian Empire*. Chicago, 1948; Strabo, *The Geography* (trans. H. L. Jones), 8 vols. London, 1961; Xenophon, *Anabasis* (The

Persian Expedition) [trans. R. Warner]. London, 1975; Plutarch, *Lives* (Dryden trans.), 6 vols. New York, 1898; M. I. Rostovtzeff, *Social and Economic History of the Roman Empire*. 2 vols. Oxford, 1957 and his *Social and Economic History of the Hellenistic World*. 3 vols. Oxford, 1941; J. B. Bury, *History of Greece to the Death of Alexander*. London, 1955; N. Garsoian, *Armenia Between Byzantium and the Sasanians*. London, 1985; N. Garsoian, *The Paulician Heresy*. The Hague, 1967; N. Garsoian, et. al. eds., *East of Byzantium: Syria and Armenia in the Formative Period*. Washington, D.C., 1982; J. Russell, *Zoroastrianism in Armenia*. Cambridge, Mass., 1987; C. G. Starr, *A History of the Ancient World*. New York, 1974.

On the History of Georgia and Caucasian Albania, see:
W. E. D. Allen, *A History of the Georgian People*. New York, 1971; and D. M. Lang, *The Georgians*. New York, 1966; *The History of the Caucasian Albanians by Movses Daskhurantsi* (translated by C. J. F. Dowsett). London, 1961.

On the History of the Armenian Church and the Christian Churches of the East, see:
M. Azarya, *The Armenian Quarter of Jerusalem*. Berkeley, 1984; M. Ormanian, *The Church of Armenia*. New York, 1988; K. Sarkissian, *The Council of Chalcedon and the Armenian Church*. New York, 1975; A. J. Arberry, ed., *Religion in the Middle East* (2 vols.). Cambridge, 1969; J. L. Gonzalez, *A History of Christian Thought* (2 vols.). New York, 1971;

On the History of Byzantium and the Armenians in the Byzantine Empire, see:
S. Der Nersessian, *Armenia and the Byzantine Empire*. Cambridge, 1965; N. Adontz, *Armenia in the Period of Justinian: The Political Conditions Based on the Naxarar System* (translated with commentary by N. Garsoian). Lisbon, 1970; P. Charanis, *The Armenians in the Byzantine Empire*. Lisbon, 1963; G. Ostrogorsky, *History of the Byzantine State*. New Brunswick, 1969; S. Runciman, *Byzantine Style and Civilization*. Penguin Books, 1975 and his *Byzantine Civilization*. Cleve-

land, 1967; A. A. Vasiliev, *History of the Byzantine Empire* (2 vols.). Madison, 1952.

On the History of the Arabs, Islam and the Bagratuni period, see:
The Cambridge History of Islam (2 vols). Cambridge, 1970; A. Hourani, *A History of the Arab Peoples*. Cambridge, Mass., 1991; V. Minorsky, *A History of Sharvan and Darband in the 10th-11th Centuries*. Cambridge, 1958 and his *Studies in Caucasian History*. London, 1953; A. Ter-Ghewondyan, *The Arab Emirates in Bagratid Armenia* (Translated with Commentary by N. Garsoian). Lisbon, 1976; C. Toumanoff, "Armenia and Georgia," in *Cambridge Medieval History* (vol 4 pt. 1); S. Lane-Poole, *A History of Egypt in the Middle Ages*. New York, 1969.

On the History of the Crusades and Cilician Armenia, see:
P. Z. Bedoukian, *Coinage of Cilician Armenia*, New York, 1962; K. M. Setton, ed., *A History of the Crusades* (6 vols.). Madison, 1969-1990, see especially S. Der Nersessian's chapter, "The Kingdom of Cilician Armenia," in vol. 2; T. S. R. Boase, ed., *The Cilician Kingdom of Armenia*. Edinburgh, 1978; A. Maalouf, *The Crusades Through Arab Eyes*. New York, 1984; S. Runciman, *A History of the Crusades* (3 vols.), New York, 1964; Hetoum, *A Lytell Cronycle* (Translated by Richard Pynson). Toronto, 1988; *La Chronique Attribuée au Connétable Smbat* (Translated by Gerard Dédéyan), Paris, 1980; G. G. Mikaelian, *History of the Cilician Armenian State* (in Russian), Yerevan, 1952; W. H. Rudt-Collenberg, *The Rupenides, The Hethumides and Lusignans. The Structure of the Armenian-Cilician Dynasties*. Paris, 1963.

On the History of Armenia from the Eleventh to the Sixteenth Centuries, see:
The best work on Armenia during the Turco-Mongol period, as well as the source frequently consulted for the final chapter of this study, is R. G. Bedrosian's, *The Turco-Mongol Invasions and the Lords of Armenia in the 13-14th Centuries* (Columbia University doctoral dissertation, 1979); other sources include, W. Barthold, *Turkestan Down to the Mongol Invasion*. London, 1968; C. Cahen, *Pre-Ottoman Turkey*. New York, 1968; D. Morgan, *Medieval Persia, 1040-1797*. London, 1988;

H. Inalcik, *The Ottoman Empire: The Classical Age, 1300-1600*. London, 1973; T. Grousset, *The Empire of the Steppes*. New Brunswick, 1970; P. Wittek, *The Rise of the Ottoman Empire*. London, 1971; J. J. Saunders, *The History of the Mongol Conquests*. London, 1971; B. Spuler, *The Mongols in History*. New York, 1971; S. Vryonis, *The Decline of Medieval Hellenism in Asia Minor and the Process of Islamization from the Eleventh to the Fifteenth Century* (Los Angeles, 1971); J. E. Woods, *The Aqquyunlu: Clan, Confederation, Empire: A Study in 15/9th-Century Turko-Iranian Politics*. Minneapolis, 1976.

On Trade, Art, Literature, and Architecture , see:
P. Arzoumanian, *Armenian Churches* (in Armenian, Russian, and English). Lisbon (n.d.).; L. Azarian, *Armenian Khatchkars* (in Armenian, Russian, and English), Lisbon (n.d.); S. Der Nersessian, *The Armenians*. New York, 1970; S. Der Nersessian, *Armenian Art*. Paris (n.d.); P. Donabedian and J. Thierry, *Armenian Art* (New York, 1989); L. A. Durnovo, *Studies in the Fine Arts of Medieval Armenia* (in Russian). Moscow, 1979; T. F. Mathews and A. K. Sanjian, *Armenian Gospel Iconography: The Tradition of the Glajor Gospel*. Washington, D.C., 1991; A. A. Novello, *The Armenians*. New York, 1986; D. Der Hovanessian and M. Margossian tr. and eds., *Anthology of Armenian Poetry*. New York, 1978; H. A. Manandian, *The Trade and Cities of Armenia in Relation to Ancient World Trade* (English translation and commentary by N. G. Garsoian). Lisbon, 1965.

Index

(b) Places, Dynasties, Peoples, Titles, Tribes, Histories, etc.

Lone College